Clericalism
The Death of Priesthood

George B. Wilson, S.J.

LITURGICAL PRESS
Collegeville, Minnesota

www.litpress.org

1   2   3   4   5   6   7   8   9

Library of Congress Cataloging-in-Publication

Wilson, George B., 1928–
   Clericalism : the death of priesthood / George B. Wilson.
     p. cm.
   ISBN-13: 978-0-8146-2945-1
   1. Priesthood—Catholic Church.   I. Title.
   BX1912.W525 2007
   262'.142—dc22   2007018975

For Anne,
sister and best friend

You, however, are "a chosen race, a royal priesthood, a people he claims for his own to proclaim the glorious works" of the One who called you from darkness into his marvelous light.

1 Peter 2:9

Since culture is a human creation and is therefore marked by sin, it too needs to be "healed, ennobled and perfected."

John Paul II, *Redemptoris Missio*

Contents

Preface   ix

Introduction: "Priest" and "Cleric":
                  Clarifying the Terminology   xiii

Part I: Cultures, Clergies, and the Ordained

Chapter 1: Clerical Cultures and How They "Work"   3

Chapter 2: Priesting Before Clergyhood   37

Chapter 3: When Priests Become Ordained Clergy   49

Part II: Tragedy and Transformation

Chapter 4: The Sexual Abuse Tragedy
                  and the Clergies that Enacted It   63

Chapter 5: Transformation:
                  Re-priesting a Clericalized Church   96

Chapter 6: Expectations of the Ordained and the Laity   110

Conclusion   149

Suggestions for Group Study   153

Acknowledgments   157

Preface

After reading a first draft of this work, a friendly Jesuit advisor made the wise suggestion that it would help you, my readers, if I were to begin by telling you some of my personal story. It could provide some illuminating context for the ideas and recommendations I am offering here.

As for the bare-bones essentials, this is the way I wrote my brief biography a few years ago: *"A priest for more than forty years. A Jesuit for more than fifty. Somewhat over seventy trying to live up to my baptism, and a few weeks longer than that sharing in the continuing gift of creation along with the rest of this mysterious universe. That's in ascending order of significance, in case you hadn't noticed."* In other words, my identity as priest and membership in the Jesuits are subordinate to the gift of baptism and the sheer dignity of being God's creation.

Today I would agree with this assessment and only need to ratchet up the numbers a bit. But skeletons call out for flesh and sinews if they are to become dialogue partners. So, for the purpose of our time together, I need to tell you a bit more of what I have been up to during these wonder-filled years of my ministry as one of the ordained.

First, during two years of studies at the Gregorian University in Rome that ended with a doctoral degree, my concentration was on the way the church's teaching on papal infallibility had been understood by the great Dominican theologians of the fourteenth–sixteenth centuries. Then I spent eleven years teaching Jesuit seminarians at Woodstock College, focusing on our understanding of the church and its sacraments, with a special eye on the day-to-day living out of those understandings by the faithful in the pews. That remains the lodestar around which my spirit and reflection have continued to orbit to this day.

If my intellectual life had followed its presumed trajectory, I would have spent a lifetime in academia as a seminary professor. But that was not to be. At the close of Vatican II the conciliar *periti* John Courtney Murray and Gustav Weigel returned to join us on the Woodstock faculty. They urged the seminary to open its doors to seminars that would help to disseminate what had happened at the council, to American priests, religious men and women, and laity. Their recommendations were accepted. The first summer institutes were mounted in 1966, and I was assigned to organize the sessions and serve as their ecclesiastical cruise director.

It is only in hindsight that I realize how profoundly those events changed the way I saw things I'd been looking at all my life. Here was the church, and its sacramental life, *occurring,* in Technicolor. Not a static reality to be merely intellectually unpacked, but a living organism in which you and I—some of us ordained and most not—were participating. We were shaping it as baptized peers. For all its roots in a divine impulse, the church was nonetheless an organism, fully human and subject to the same dynamics that come to expression in any human institution, including its warts and sins. If we do not learn to love the church in its sinfulness, we will not love the church loved by the Lord but, rather, some figment of our romantic imagination. (Thank you, Henri DeLubac.)

I spent three summers guiding the program. Then in the succeeding two years my engagement with the embodied reality of the unfolding church continued, as Woodstock's coordinator for two historic seminars. One was for 135 women religious, superiors, or spiritual directors engaged in the formation of their members. The second was a similar event, perhaps even more significant in light of the tectonic plates being shifted. It involved the same number of contemplative women from across the great traditions of the church: Carmelites, Poor Clares, Passionists, Redemptoristines, Trappistines, and Benedictines. Some of them had not crossed the threshold of their cloister in forty years. The meeting, which had started with an open agenda, ended in the creation of a national organization, the Association of Contemplative Sisters. That body continues today, supporting the contemplative life of its members, now both canonical and laywomen.

My role in those seminars led in turn to thirty-four years as a staff member at Management Design Institute. There our dominant clientele consisted of religious congregations, dioceses, and Protestant judicatories. Serving as process facilitators and planning mentors, we helped hundreds of groups to tap into the power of their founding vision as they translated that vision into more effective ways of living the Gospel in a changed world. Our focus was always on the way human systems—including religious ones—actually "work." Each has its own absolutely unique myth and culture, but, as they try to bring their vision to life, common principles of human organization come into play. Looking back on the experience I realize that it was a great grace to walk intimately with such a rich diversity of manifestations of the reality we so glibly label "the church." I found myself in the company of Francis of Assisi and Benedict and Dominic; of Mother Guerin and Catherine McCauley and Marguerite Bourgeois; of Isaac Hecker and Edmund Rice—with occasional brushes with Martin Luther and John Wesley. It was sacred ground.

Yet my story would not be complete without a complementary reality, my sharing in liturgical worship with two special communities. I spent every Christmas with the Medical Mission Sisters in Philadelphia; every Holy Week with the community of the Grail outside Cincinnati. Both communities have a profound sense of biblical prayer and embodied ritual. And for over twenty-five years I have had, and continue to have, the rich experience of presiding regularly at liturgy within two African-American parishes in Cincinnati. Praying with them, sharing the Word with them, and feasting with them has nourished my soul with the wine of the Spirit in ways I am sure are beyond my fathoming.

It is that body of experiences that grounds the reflections in this work. My exploration of the sad reality of clericalism calls for naming uncomfortable, perhaps even hard, realities. I name them, not as an indictment of any individual cleric or layperson. In my work I have interacted with great numbers of the faithful, both ordained and not, who have remained priestly and uninfected by clericalism. They are a blessing in our church community. What I have tried to name is rather a seduction that carries its own allure for every last one of us, ordained or lay. Our love for this warty old church demands of us that we recognize clericalism where it exists, and work against it in favor of the priesthood to which we are called by virtue of our baptism.

In the chapters that follow, after some preliminary reflections on our confused terminology and the nature of culture, I invite the reader to ponder in succession (1) the culture of clergyhood; (2) the nature of priesting; (3) the clericalization of priests; (4) the role played by the clerical culture in the collective tragedy of the sexual abuse situation; and (5) the transformation that will be required if we are to be true to our common vocation as a priestly people.

And so to our topic.

Introduction
"Priest" and "Cleric": Clarifying the Terminology

A common mantra concerning the scandal of sexual abuse by Roman Catholic priests pinpoints "the clerical culture" as the root cause of what went terribly wrong.

Of course each individual abusing priest had his own personal story of sexual underdevelopment and psychological disorder, his own uniquely manifested need for power. And the same is true of the bishops. The leadership failure of each individual bishop who moved abusing priests from one assignment to another was grounded in his own personal story. That story manifested its own particular combination of ignorance, naiveté, and less-than-admirable motivations such as fear and self-interest. But when the same kind of behaviors show up in so many individuals in so many different settings within the same organization, we naturally look for common causative factors. We look for factors that go toward explaining the behaviors of the system as a whole. According to the prevailing assessment, the reality that links this tragic story together is a shared bundle of elements which add up to a "clerical culture." From the perspective of a culture, what took place was not a series of isolated, unrelated tragedies. They were all part of a single, coherent drama.

It is a plausible interpretation. Commonalities in behavior do beg for the naming of shared factors to account for them. But naming the common root cause will contribute little to our understanding, and much less to healing and transformation, if we simply apply a label and let it go at that.

Moralizing about the evil clerical culture may be psychologically satisfying, but merely indulging ourselves in moralizing will lead only to further frustration. An unhealthy system—and the clerical culture is unhealthy—will always prove itself impervious to outrage unless it is accompanied by further critical analysis. Rage is by its nature transitory. For genuine change new modes of relating are required, and if we are to create them we need insight into the mindsets and attitudes that gave rise to the present unhealthy system in the first place. If we are to enlarge our insight and thereby discover the best steps for forestalling repetition of the tragedy, we need to dig deeper. We need to mine the implications of each of the two terms in vogue. Just what is involved when you deal with a "culture"? And what goes into making something "clerical"?

A Linguistic and Conceptual Muddle

Before we reflect on the nature of cultures, however, we need to listen to the way we use terms in our everyday speech. A common headline offers a starting point. The headline in a representative diocesan newspaper seems innocuous enough: *"Clergy of the Diocese Meet at Renewal Center; Priests to Discuss Confirmation Norms."* Similar articles, with more or less the same headlines, have appeared many times over the years.

Why should a line like that raise eyebrows? What could possibly be amiss in such a straightforward headline? A lot, as it turns out. And the consequences contain a whole bundle of mischief for our church and our understanding of what our God is about.

The fact that such texts do not give us pause is itself an indicator of a serious issue. No red flags are raised. The dog didn't bark. We have become so accustomed to this kind of language that we do not even remark on the confusion that it perpetuates. It serves as our ecclesiastical wallpaper.

Read the headline again. What is the issue lurking behind this boilerplate way of speaking? To mix a metaphor: what elephant is staring us in the face? The answer is: the implied *identification* of "clergy" with "priest."

You're not alone if you don't see the problem with this identification. You might be thinking: "But aren't they the same thing? Aren't the two terms just synonyms for each other? Aren't all priests clergy, and all clergy priests? Wait a minute! Deacons are considered clergy and they aren't ordained priests. Is that the problem?"

Well, no, although it's a start. The issue shows up when priests gather for a "clergy meeting" and the deacons (who are ordained and recognized by society as clergy) are not included. Some noses can get slightly bent out of shape at what is experienced as an unwarranted form of exclusion. Are deacons in the circle or not?

The water becomes even murkier when people raise the question of whether religious sisters or brothers are clergy or not. From a canonical perspective, such non-ordained religious are not clergy. But those canonical niceties matter little to laypeople. They generally tend to put all these people in the same mental bin: "Official religious folk." And that everyday mentality is far more powerful, more telling, than canonical definitions.

But these issues of turf and inclusion aren't the real fly in the chrism. They actually get in the way of uncovering the more significant confusion at work. They serve to mask the issue that is latent in the headline.

No, the real issue is not who gets lumped in the clergy bin or who gets to attend clergy gatherings. The much more significant issue lies in the fact that the identification of priests with clergy involves mixing—confusing—two radically different orders of *reality.* "Priest" is a religious term, pointing us to the transcendent or numinous or sacred dimension of life, to the holy. "Clergy" is a sociological term that names the fact that society recognizes a certain segment of its members as having recognizable social features and norms that distinguish them from the rest of society. When we confuse these two orders of reality by interchanging the two terms we implicitly ratify the notion that priestly activity is the prerogative only of these individuals socially recognized by their ordination. Priestly—sacred—activity is the preserve of the ordained; laity need not apply. By continuing to make our clergy the only manifestations of priestliness, we reduce our lay faithful to passive recipients of the holy actions of the ordained, diminishing the dignity that should rightly be theirs by virtue of their baptism and confirmation.

Once we begin to appreciate that these are two very different orders of reality, the religious and the sociological, it becomes possible to entertain some potentially rich alternatives and questions. The answers to them might call all of us to some costly conversions:

1) Is it possible to be ordained "clergy" without being "priest"? *Yes.*
2) Is it possible to be "priest" without being "clergy"? *Yes.*
3) If the two realities can exist independently of one another, can they coexist in the same human person? *Yes. "Priest" and "cleric" don't necessarily exclude one another. In fact, we hope that all our clergy are priests—even those we label deacons, bishops, sisters, and brothers. But, as we will see in chapter 2, they aren't the only priests in the congregation.*

I realize that these three points may be confusing or even disconcerting to my readers at this stage. A full grasp of their intent depends on further explanation in coming chapters. At the moment I am compelled to use a bit of linguistic jujitsu, using customary words in uncustomary ways, in order to open the possibility of new insight and better responses to our situation.

New Terminology

In this book I will be using some turns of language that can with some accuracy (or even disdain) be called neologisms. Readers may be put off when I speak of "priesting" or "clergifying." However, I speak this way not out of a desire to be catchy or cute, but because of a profound conviction. Unless we wrestle with new forms of expression in order to tap into the energies of new insights, the language of the past will continue to trap us within its walls. As long as we remain within the confines of our habitual forms of expression, our understanding (and therefore our behavior) will not change. After all, the words we use reinforce the way we see the world. Our terms make us comfortable that the way things are is the way they're meant to be. And it is precisely that comfort which blocks the impulse to take a hard look at the present disorder and enter into the work of changing it.

My claim is that our ways of speaking perpetuate an unacknowledged muddle that results from identifying "priest" as "clergy." That inappropriate identification has allowed unhealthy behaviors to cloud the image and diminish the power of the Christian faith in our world. If we continue to *talk* in a certain way, we will also continue to *act* in the ways that those expressions have made comfortable. And as a result we will perpetuate some bad stuff.

By this point it will be obvious to the reader that I have laid on myself a heavy burden. I am challenging our traditional forms of speech and charging them with being manifestations of muddled thinking, leading to questionable attitudes and behaviors. That makes it incumbent on me to spell out clearly just what is involved in the religious world of priesting as contrasted with the sociological world of clergifying.

Incidentally, I should say that I am under no illusion that I will be able to change our habitual modes of expression. People will continue to use "priest" and "clergy" interchangeably even if my writing succeeds beyond my wildest imagining. King Canute will succeed in talking down the waves before such a transformation of usage takes place.

No, my goal in putting these thoughts together is at once more modest and perhaps more difficult. My hope is that after mulling over what I am trying to say, when you or I do use the word "priest" when we mean "clergy" or vice versa, it will be with a slight hitch. A momentary stop, where these thoughts can serve as a brake and make us ask, "Is this what I really want to say? Or does my new framing of the question compel me to struggle for new words, new forms of expression? Are there things I want to change in our understanding of the holy? Behaviors I want to reject?"

My purpose in writing, however, also is not because I'm a stickler for using proper language when naming things. Developing clearer concepts and language to express them is only the necessary first step. The goal is to articulate a vision and think through the steps required to create a whole new set of attitudes and mutual relationships between the ordained and the Catholic laity.[1]

The foundational insight which clamors for explanation is, as I have indicated, that we are dealing with two distinct realities when we use the terms "clergy" (a sociological perspective) and "priest" (a religious one). Let me tip my hand and indicate where we are heading: there are other clergies than that of the ordained ministers (chapter 1) and other priests than the ordained (chapter 2). We will eventually focus on the ordained and the way they and the rest of the faithful relate to each other (chapters 3–6), but the effort can't succeed if we begin there. The destructive phenomenon of clericalism in the church is only one manifestation of a human disorder that infects many areas of society. It cannot be properly understood if we see it as something which occurs *only* in the church.

We have to begin, not with the ordained ministers we traditionally have called "priests" and church folk called "the laity" but with clergy groups in general, and the relationship of each to its corresponding laity. Only after that foundation is laid will we be in a position to appreciate the unique features of the relationship between church ministers and the faithful. Even prior to that, we need to put into place some foundational notions about cultures in general. After we have taken those two steps we will be in a position to explore effectively what is amiss in the relationship between the ordained and the lay faithful with an eye to proposing specific strategies for changing the present disordered relationship.

So we turn to cultures.

---

1. Protestant readers will easily recognize that the issues addressed here apply in their religious world as well.

Cultures, Clergies, and the Ordained

Chapter One
Clerical Cultures
and How They "Work"

What Makes a Culture?

In recent years the field of cultures has been treated extensively
in a great variety of disciplines. It is beyond the scope of this small
book to attempt to summarize that broad exploration. For our
purposes a few key points from the ongoing conversation will
suffice.

Culture is an embodied drama

For human-systems practitioners it is a given that a culture is,
first of all, not some sort of conceptual abstraction. The word may
be abstract, but the reality is always embodied. A culture is something quite distinct from the ways we think or talk about it. It involves very concrete patterns of behavior and ways of thinking
that give shape to a particular body of people—whether we can
put names on those features or not. Culture comes to expression
in the story of a people. And that story is a *single drama being
enacted by a specific set of players* within a broader historical
context. It has its specific shape because of a deep and commonly
held set of standards and expectations which come to expression
in the behaviors of the collection of players. A culture is a power-
filled reality that conditions the ways the people in a given social
system will tend to think and behave. The menu of options for
action available to us as humans is limited by the cultural forces

which have shaped and imprinted us. Living out of a culture, with its innumerable assumptions and expectations, inevitably evokes in us a challenge when we come face-to-face with persons operating out of a different one: we find it difficult to understand their behavior because we don't know where it's coming from. We get our "scripts" from the cultures that have shaped us.

Immigrants, for example, as they try to adapt to a new culture learn that fact immediately; their customary ways of behaving, learned in the old country, are clearly out of place in the new. They've walked onto a new stage with furniture in strange places, and they don't know what their lines are within the story being enacted there. The inhabitants of, say, Lapland can't by a simple act of will begin acting like Neapolitans; they lack the expected script and gestures.[1]

Cultures are generated out of a complex mix of factors. Ann Swidler offers a good working list: "symbolic vehicles of meaning, including beliefs, ritual practices, art forms, and ceremonies, as well as informal . . . practices such as language, gossip, stories, and rituals of daily life."[2] Her list alerts us to the fact that the full power of a culture cannot be captured by noting only the components of group life that are formalized and articulated. The official proclamations of the group, for example its mission statements and other policy declarations, provide only a fraction of the material needed to appreciate its culture. To understand Americans, for example, the Declaration of Independence is not a bad start, but it tells us nothing about how we Americans actually *live* what it professes. Much of what gives shape and power to a particular culture is not recognized in formal declarations but is revealed in the daily, informal interactions of its members.

---

1. For an extended analysis of culture as drama, see Hugh Dalziel Duncan, *Symbols in Society* (NY: Oxford University Press, 1968).

2. Quoted in Michael Paul Gallagher, S.J., *Clashing Cymbals: An Introduction to Faith and Culture* (NY: Paulist Press, 2003), 19. See also Thomas Clarke, *Playing in the Gospel* (Kansas City: Sheed & Ward, 1968), 164-66.

Cultures express themselves in everyday behavior

Not only is much of the reality informal and (only apparently) trivial and transitory, but also the actual workings of a culture, its operating dynamics, are largely *unconscious,* not easily accessible even to those who live it out each day of their lives. It was only when the first sea animals crawled out of the ocean and looked back that they discovered water. We all swim in, and act out of, attitudes and assumptions whose influence and origins escape our detection. We imitate the behaviors of others who were significant members of our daily context of life without being aware that we are doing so. We take on and live out loyalties without being able to account rationally for them. (Only at this late stage of my life am I aware that I hitch my pants up the same way my father did. How did *that* get transmitted?) The genesis of a culture is based on *mimesis,* on bodily mirroring the behaviors of significant figures in the group, rather than reasoning from commonly held principles. In large areas of our lives we act the way we do because we have taken on the beliefs, attitudes, and behaviors of people who held significance for us. Why else would anyone ever root for the Yankees?

Cultures are both empowering and limiting

Our cultural heritage tells us what to value, how to behave, and to whom we should listen and attend. Those promptings are like an internal compass or road map. They go a long way toward enabling us to navigate our way through the otherwise daunting array of options available to us in life. In that sense they empower us, because much of what impels us to act in this world has already been supplied for us by the cultures within which we have been embedded since childhood. A homely example: the members of my family are acutely aware of how different we siblings are one from another, but ask any outsider and they are likely to say, "Oh, you know those Wilsons, they're all alike!"

But by the same token, every culture creates limits. The limits apply in the first instance to what we can *imagine.* The expected attitudes and behaviors of a particular culture can be so powerful that it becomes all but impossible for its members to even conceive of other ways of being. (Think of those Laplanders trying to figure out what Neapolitan hand gestures mean.) The culture becomes, in effect, a set of prejudgments imprinted in the psyche, making other ways of organizing life appear not just as other but as threats to the stability generated by the normative culture. If not resisted, those other ways of being can cause us to lose the security we enjoy because of a set of long-accepted beliefs and attitudes.

Michael Paul Gallagher describes this feature as the "doubleness" inherent in every culture. "[A culture] involves observable practices or socially legitimated ways of acting but it also entails a more concealed set of subjective attitudes often assimilated unconsciously over a long time. Together these habits of acting and of interpreting can either imprison people within prejudices or they can become avenues towards authentic living, towards self-transcending choices that challenge the negative bias of any culture."[3]

We are all responsible for our cultures

The story of a culture may appear on the surface to be a series of actions taken and monologues voiced only by the lead players. They are the members of the guild who appear to control the workings of the whole. They are the individuals whose names usually appear in the written narrative of the group. (As others have noted, many a history starts out with the intent of telling the story of a people and ends by narrating the story of its kings and generals.) But such a view leaves out the role being played by the Greek chorus made up of the host of the unnamed, the role that gives legitimacy to the roles of those in the spotlight. The stars may enjoy power in the system, but they do so only to the extent that the rest of the undifferentiated players allow it, for whatever reason or (unacknowledged) motive.

---

3. Gallagher, *Clashing Cymbals*, 24.

A culture can survive only if it is nurtured by zillions of tiny behavioral interactions among all or almost all of those implicated in the culture. If we may continue the metaphor of games, that means that cultures are generated and maintained by *all the players* in the system. To apply this insight to our present concern: it would be a fatal mistake to view a clerical culture as being generated only by its clergy. Like any other culture, the clerical culture is the product of everyone affected by—or implicated in—its continuance. That includes equally those who are seen as laypeople vis-à-vis a particular body of clergy. Cultures are generated by the behavioral interactions *between* a particular clergy and its corresponding laity. The generation and continuance of a culture is a matter of relationships, a single reality mutually created by both sets of participants.

To refer once again to the current tragedy: for many people, to place the responsibility for the sexual misconduct at the foot of a clerical culture seems to translate simply into assigning all responsibility *only* to the ordained: the bishops and priests. It's a short-sighted view. To take that tack would mean adopting the nonproductive policy named so aptly in the '60s, when transactional analysis was in vogue. One of the games was called "Get the Leader." The name of the game pointed to our human propensity for absolving ourselves of the burden of complicity in bad outcomes by putting all the responsibility on persons in leadership positions. Playing "Get the Leader"—in this instance, blaming the bishops—is an easy out, a form of cheap grace. Rabbi Abraham Heschel made the point very succinctly in his oft-quoted dictum: in a free society "some are guilty but all are responsible."

Cultures, and the relationships through which they are enacted, create a world of meaning for their adherents. Cultures benefit peoples' interests or they would not survive. That includes, in the instance of a clerical culture, not only the members who manifestly enjoy the benefits produced by the whole network of beliefs and behaviors that create and maintain the culture. It embraces all those among the laity who covertly derive rewards from playing their prescribed roles in the single drama. Paradoxically, it includes even those laity who at a certain level are actually being harmed by the system. The harm may take the form of economic injustice: clerics living high among an impoverished laity. It may consist in unwarranted exclusion of the laity from reasonable empowerment: their life experience is treated as insignificant by the clergy, even in matters of great moment. It can mean that in a significant area of life (such as their relationship to God) they forego, quite unconsciously, their potential for growth, regressing to a state of unwarranted dependency when in every other dimension of their lives they function as quite mature adults. In any case they sustain the prevailing pattern by accepting the script the culture assigns to them. The unacknowledged benefit they derive from acquiescing to a diminished role outweighs the diminishment they might not even be aware of. Otherwise, they would take action to change not only the particular lines but the very balance of roles that enacts the present drama.

Cultures are highly resistant to change

Finally, cultures cling to existence tenaciously, for at least two reasons implied in what we have noted so far. The first lies precisely in the fact that much of their causation is unacknowledged. The scripts by which the single drama is enacted have been recited so long that they have become second nature to the participants. The clerical culture in the church, for example, is actually a complex of set speeches, *sotto voce* asides, soliloquies, incoherent crowd sounds, and behavioral tics, all occurring simultaneously on multiple stages—in the chancery, yes, but also in the parish, and in the homes of parishioners.

The second reason for the tenacity of any culture lies in its capacity to generate meaning. We recite the lines given to us because to risk changing them could disrupt the whole story that creates order in the midst of the chaos of life. Organizing life in a particular manner, as noted above, provides security. Cultures give us roots and identity. It is easy to call for cultural change. But to bring it about requires letting go of the present security arising from a clear plot, distinct roles, and acceptable lines, for a set of future cultural forms whose disconcerting effect on our lives cannot be fully anticipated. For the individual who risks acting out a different paradigm, the cost in terms of rejection by the players who want to continue with the reassuring story may be high. And that letting go will only have the desired effect when the accumulation of tiny individual countercultural actions is sufficient to become a catalytic mass—a "tipping point" in the current idiom—that can prevail over the comfort of the status quo.

What Makes a Clergy?

With these admittedly inadequate observations on the nature and implications of cultures in general, we turn our attention to the specific culture out of which the misconduct situation arose. What does it mean to be clergy?

A brief reminder may be in order. As we saw in the introduction, the words "priest" and "clergy" are often used indiscriminately. *Webster's New 20th Century Dictionary of the English Language* illustrates this usage by defining clergy as "men ordained for religious service, as ministers, priests, etc., collectively." That is a knot we will have to untie in the coming chapters. It will not be easy, because we have been conditioned for a long time to move back and forth between the words "clergy" and "priest" as if the realities they represent were identical: a priest is always clergy; clergy are always ordained. It will require serious intellectual discipline to remind ourselves that each time I refer to clergy in the course of our reflections I am not necessarily speaking of ordained priests. Nor am I automatically speaking of the ordained even when I refer to priesthood. Without that effort, old mental habits will take over and we will slide back into the confusion we are attempting to unravel.

We begin the unraveling process with a straightforward statement: A cleric need not be a priest. Nor need he be a deacon, or ordained for that matter. Clergyhood, it turns out, need have nothing to do with religion at all. As noted in the introduction, clergy is not a religious but rather a sociological reality and designation. It is true that the reality of clergyhood sometimes *manifests itself in* men and women who happen also to be ordained ministers, religious persons. But we need to hold that fact at arm's length while we examine the nature of clergyhood in general.

It may perhaps help the reader if I jump immediately to the concrete before attempting to further define clergy. Under the umbrella of "clergy" I will be referring to professional groups such as lawyers, physicians, academics, generals—and, yes, priests, ministers, and rabbis. As we move on and gradually put flesh on the criterion for inclusion as clergy, there may be still other groupings that might warrant the designation, but for the present I will limit my analysis to these long-standing professions.

Clergyhood is essential to organizational development

Why might these groups be lumped under the term "clergy"? What leads a society to designate an identified body of its citizens as clergy? The identification of a particular group of people as clergy is part of the differentiating process of organizational development in any society. From an initial "amoebic" or undifferentiated state, groups transform themselves into one of increased complexity and stratification. I would describe the process in the following way:

a) In a society which was heretofore undifferentiated in this particular manner,

b) a process takes place through which a particular collection of individuals begins to be seen and related to as a class

c) on the basis of a recognition and acceptance that this collection of individuals possesses special access to powers not available in the same way to the members of the society in general;

d) the power is most often associated with a body of knowledge or competence held by the initiates,

e) knowledge or competence judged by the general membership to be of great significance for the life of the society,

f) and because the members of the society are unable for whatever reason to access the knowledge or competence themselves, they are willing to acknowledge the credentials of the
particular collection of individuals and confer on them status
and privileges not accorded to others in the society.

As the organizational development of any organism proceeds,
differentiation of needs is a common experience. Members of the
society gradually become more conscious that they have common
needs intrinsic to their survival as a society. A society needs its
members to be physically and mentally healthy. We need ordered
processes for adjudicating between competing claims in our collective life. We need methods for determining the credibility of
knowledge claims that are put forward for our human growth and
action. We need a reasonably secure world. And the society (or
at least some subgroups within it) needs structures to assure
collective wisdom regarding the nature of transcendent reality and
the rituals by which they acknowledge relationship to that transcendent realm. By dint of experience, societies come to recognize
that certain individuals are somehow endowed with special gifts
that contribute to these facets of the common good.

Some people give evidence of the gift of healing, and societies
recognize and give legitimacy to all sorts of healthcare practitioners, from witch doctors to physicians. Others are skilled at making the fine distinctions required for prudential judgment
concerning the balance between the common good and individual
rights and interests, and society generates a legal elite. Others
display wisdom in analyzing competing truth claims, and we get
the scholarly guilds. Some know how to mobilize a society in order
to defend itself from attack, and so the society begins to recognize
public safety professionals and the military. And some are recognized for their ability to proclaim or articulate people's beliefs
about the transcendent or for their ability to lead the ritualization
of those beliefs, and so we get priests, ministers, rabbis, imams,
and shamans.

Those varied gifts are attributed to the accumulation of specialized bodies of knowledge or wisdom: medical, legal, scholarly,

military, or spiritual. In the early stages of societal development it is unimportant where or how the gifts originate within an individual; it is enough that others come to realize the value of the particular gifts and recognize their presence in certain individuals within the social system. Individuals who give evidence of possessing those gifts then begin to be treated differently. At a later stage it is recognized that the phenomenon is not restricted to individuals. The same gift is recognized in different individuals, even when they are not actually exercising that particular gift. The society begins to develop nomenclature that corresponds to its recognition of this repeated phenomenon. A name is assigned, a class is constituted: physician, lawyer, scholar, soldier, minister. The different treatment accorded to members of the class begins to be stylized and turned into custom. A clergy has been created.

People who are familiar with the dynamics of organizational development might be willing to accept what has been said thus far. It is a legitimate way of looking at the development of some quite powerful and valued *professions* in society. But why call them *clergy?* What is the warrant for such a usage?

At this point we need to leave aside the concrete groupings we have been considering and turn our attention to terminology, and specifically to the common root behind words like "clergy," "clerical," "clerk," and "clericalism." The Greek or Latin or Arabic roots of contemporary terms frequently direct our attention to experiences that occasioned the formation of a word. They point us to meanings that lie dormant within our everyday usage but are still able to shed light on what we are communicating. In some instances they may contribute to quite important elements of meaning.

The first thing we have to confront is that in its roots the notion of the *kleros* has no intrinsic relation to religion or the holy. The *Oxford English Dictionary* informs us that a *kleros* was a "lot, an allotment, a piece of land, an estate, a heritage." According to *The New Encyclopedia Britannica* (15th edition), the *cleros* was a "share, an inheritance." What was inherited, the thing shared, was quite mundane and secular: physical property. At root, clergy are propertied, people with an inheritance.

This secular meaning of *cleros* was gradually transformed by the Christian community. (If the process by which that transformation took place has not yet been researched, it is a subject for several doctoral dissertations.) The result, as *The New Encyclopedia Britannica* tells us, is that "most Christian churches, including the Roman Catholic, understand the clergy [today] as persons functioning within the priesthood of all the people but ordained, or set aside, for particular service, especially in connection with Eucharistic ministry."

That is not to say that the early church did not recognize certain individuals as exercising particular forms of service in the community. It did. But the practice of grouping them together under a single collective noun, as *kleros*, and thereby distinguishing them from an undifferentiated mass of members, is a later phenomenon, reflecting a later stage of societal development. (It should be noted that prior to that stage of development it would also be a mistake to refer to anyone as "laity." The paradox is that there was no collection called "laity" until there was a class called "clergy." As distinguishable classes they come into existence together.)

When terms from one sphere are adopted by particular communities and given new meanings, however, they do not lose all of the associations they carried in their earlier incarnations. The linguistic connections between words like "clergy," "clerk," "clerical," and "clericalism" are not accidental. These related words point to a deeper level of meaning that we should not ignore.

It is on the basis of that deeper layer of meaning that we can say ordained religious persons are not the only ones who belong to a corporate reality called "clergy." Academics are clergy; lawyers and physicians and military officers are clergy; the ordained are also clergy. At one stage of societal development the meaning of "clergy" was quite simple: first they were the landowners, then they were those who could read! Clergy are guilds within society, groupings recognized collectively as different from the rest of the populace. Each group's identity focused on a different need in the society. And the ways by which an individual is joined to, and is seen as a member of, the grouping are different for each guild.

But the fundamental point remains: you move from being one of the undifferentiated mass of citizens, you become distinct and set apart and identified with a collection of similarly recognized people, by passing through a doorway of some sort. The assessment of your worthiness to get through the door is controlled by those who are already inside. They set the criteria, and they design the training that will mold your original gifts into a shape suited to the needs of the profession.

This is not a bad thing in itself. That is an important caveat I want to make at this point. The existence of a clergy need not indicate some sort of pathology in society. Many individuals in these different manifestations of clergyhood perform outstanding service within their designated realm. Their existence, as we noted in our comments on cultures in general, provide meaning and security in a chaotic world.

Clergyhood brings genuine benefits—and harmful potential

The term "cleric," like the term "clergy," implies no value judgment. It does not carry the same negative meaning we will meet in the term "clericalism." But membership in a clergy group brings with it consequences, and not all are salutary. Some might be described as occupational hazards: the risks that accompany the benefits. It is those negative potentials we need to look at. If steps are not taken to guard against them, a positive state of clergyhood can be infected with clerical*ism*. It can become clericalized. The consequences of that disorder will not affect each individual of the guild in the same way or with the same intensity. As strong as the power of clergyhood and its potential negatives are, whether a given member remains true to its positive potential or, instead, succumbs to its attendant risks, is a matter of personal character and maturity. That said, every form of clergyhood brings with it the potential for good and harm.

We need to reflect on the effects that tend to emerge from the powerful force of clergyhood. As I name various effects in no particular order, I will also from time to time extrapolate some of the resulting clerical attitudes that may come to characterize the behavior of members of the clergy. These are realities that the member(s) of the group might never actually recognize as operative in their behavior. In fact, they might strongly disavow one or another of them. As finite and imperfect creatures we all operate out of cognitive assumptions and affective attitudes that we would disown if we were directly challenged. But those who interact with us can frequently see such attitudes manifested indirectly in our behavior. They are operative though not consciously acknowledged. Clerics are no more prone to such a disconnect between beliefs and behavior than anyone else. It's just that the nature of clergyhood gives the behaviors a more specific texture. We turn, then, to the effects that tend to arise from clergyhood.

What are the Seeds of Clericalism?

Clericalism grants automatic status

Individuals who pass the portal into a particular group of clergy take on a new identity within society in general. They are seen by others, and therefore see themselves, as imbued with the characteristics of the clerical group. The corporate identity gives to the individual an experience of inclusion within a circle that has public standing in the society.

That new identity brings with it a kind of empowerment for the individual who is legitimated by the process. Let the shingle on your door announce that you are, for example, a lawyer, and a new presumption is created. People attribute to you capabilities that are commonly associated with members of that profession. And what is crucial is that this happens before you have demonstrated any of those competencies in their personal contexts. (You may have demonstrated some such competence within the circumscribed setting of those who manage the admittance process, by passing the bar exam, for example.) Prior to any performance on your part, through their conferring of a title, you benefit from the acts of all those who have preceded you under the same title you now legitimately wear. This can give rise to one of the attitudes mentioned above. Each of them carries great power in directing behavior precisely because it is not acknowledged.

Unexamined Attitude

Clergy: "Because I belong to the clergy I am automatically credible. I don't have to earn my credibility by my performance."

Laity: "There's a diploma on the wall so I can put my trust in her (or him)."

Clergyhood's embodiments: dress and address and perks

The acceptance of a group of members as a distinctive clergy is a matter of trust given to them by those who are "lay" with regard to their particular special arena of service. The system as a whole, by a mutually shared but frequently unacknowledged process, generates a set of expectations.

However, the arrival of a clergy group does not happen only in the psychological arena of expectations and presumptions, or even in the realm of legal or canonical powers. It frequently comes to expression in the form of external symbols, such as distinctive dress, titles, and forms of address, and associations with symbolic objects. And then there are the perks accorded to the clergy.

Take garb, for example. Although in today's world academic clergy largely limit special dress to ceremonial occasions such as graduations, the professorial elite used to wear distinctive caps and gowns on a daily basis. Military personnel and public-safety personnel are of course recognized by their uniforms. To this day, in courtrooms in the British Commonwealth barristers wear wigs and ceremonial robes. In our own country, although lawyers have long relinquished any normative uniform, distinctive garb remains in the form of a judge's gown. (In the most recent past we were treated to the unilateral decision by Chief Justice Rehnquist to add those mikado stripes to his robe lest the groundlings underestimate the seriousness of a charge of impeachment—and more importantly, lest they miss the fact that he was *chief* justice. It was cause for lampoons precisely because it did *not* fit in with our otherwise egalitarian culture.) Physicians wear white coats even in circumstances where there is no particular health reason for them. And although Protestant clergy have largely abandoned distinctive dress except for those occasions when they are leading their communities in liturgical ritual, Catholic clergy retain the practice of distinguishing dress, the Roman collar, even when they are engaged in civil or secular pursuits not unique to their profession.

The word "uniform" itself may suggest some pregnant implications. It really is "*uni*-form." Its effect is to pour into the individual the powers of the group: the exact same powers enjoyed by every other member of the guild. It is at once empowering and potentially depersonalizing. The "uni" in the "form" can represent the suppression of all individuality and personhood of the wearer.

If I may share an evocative experience:

> A bishop who is a personal friend of mine had just flown home from a national meeting of Catholic bishops. When I asked him how it went, he told of the distressing experience of being "collared" by a drunken man sitting next to him on the plane. The man belabored him throughout the long flight with a monologue of his sad and guilty life. Of course, such a one-way narrative by someone in his drunken condition offered not the slightest potential for any positive change or rehabilitation, for ministry or evangelization. The bishop told me it was the last time he would wear his Roman collar in that type of setting.

Another way the distinction between the members of a clergy group and its own laity is manifested is in the way members of the profession are expected to be addressed. We have "Professor" or "Doctor Sweeney," "Colonel Schwartz," and "Father" or "Bishop O'Rourke." (Not to speak of the even more Olympian, and frequently quite insincere, designations used on *very* formal occasions, such as "Your Excellency," "The Distinguished Past President," etc.) The titles themselves stir up a whole set of attitudes and behaviors in their respective "laity."

Unexamined Attitude

Clergy: "People use a special title in addressing me, so I must be something special."

Laity: "She's got a title; I better shape up."

This may be the place to remind ourselves of what was noted about cultures in general: those who exhibit these external embodiments of clergyhood are not the only ones maintaining the system. Those who are lay with regard to that particular form of clergy not only passively support them, they may positively need them. I recall the personal experience of a wonderful Catholic bishop. He was a highly introverted man who had grown up in a very Catholic city. Suddenly he was named bishop for an area with a very small percentage of Catholics. He wanted in the worst way to have his priests see him as a person rather than as a role; he wanted them to call him by his first name. But they were very wary of his vision of church and took measures to protect themselves and keep him at arm's length. Although he desperately desired to be acknowledged for his personhood simply by having people address him by his baptismal name, the clergy would never accept him in that way. They always used his formal title, and thereby reduced him to a cutout they could gripe about—behind his back.

Another way in which the clergy-lay relationship comes to expression is in the perks or rewards granted to the clergy. Physicians have special parking places near the entrance to the hospital, which is a reasonable practice in light of emergency needs and the crucial factor of time. Pastors also often have designated places in the parking lot, with less justification. Personalized nameplates contribute to the process, as do separate dining rooms and the officers' mess on a military base. The matter may be as mundane as Father being favored over the rest of the people and escorted to the front of the line for flu shots. Although priests in Roman collars (or nuns in habits) do not routinely ride free on buses anymore, or get into movies without paying (younger Catholics may not have even heard of that old custom), state troopers may still be inclined to let them off with a warning when they have clearly been speeding.

Unexamined Attitude

Clergy: "The laity accept these manifestations of privilege so they must be deserved."

Laity: "It's showing respect for the cloth."

Each of these embodiments—dress, title, and privileges—can be harmless enough in itself. But cumulatively they can have a corrosive effect on the individual member of the clergy group. It is important to reflect on this in light of our general comments on the origins and staying power of cultures in general.

These realities are accurately named "embodiments." They occur in the arena of bodily behavior. They may never even be mentioned in the formal statements about the lofty character of the particular clergy group. For example, the mission statement of a professional organization will highlight the service its members perform, but one would search in vain for mention of their privileges. The bodily character is crucial. It makes such externalities all the more powerful because, as long-accepted "givens," they function under the radar. Cultural patterns that are unconsciously accepted by participants in the system maintain a greater hold on the psyche than its conscious rhetoric.

Perhaps the clearest insight into the actual impact of these realities was contained in a comment attributed to one of Richard Nixon's associates, trying to unravel the story of Nixon's tragic downfall. He quipped: "When they play 'Hail to the Chief,' give a twenty-one-gun salute, and everybody stands up when you come into the room, and nobody ever tells you to go to hell, you lose touch with reality."

"You lose touch with reality." What a devastating assessment. One of the manifestations of that slide into unreality happens when the individual cleric begins to consider the perks and shows of deference as entitlements. What originated as a graceful offering by the laity is transmuted in the psyche of the cleric and becomes a claim. It takes little more for it to become a demand required of one's "station"—regardless of one's performance.

Unexamined Attitude

Clergy: "We deserve any privilege the laity seem to want to give us."

Laity: "It's a harmless little custom."

There is a great irony here. When these manifestations of clergy-hood show up in the arena of the Christian community, we encounter what would seem to be an embarrassing disconnect. Did not the Jesus of the gospels take a quite clear stance against exactly these forms of distinction? In the twenty-third chapter of Matthew he may be denouncing the teachers of the law of his own day, but it would not seem unwarranted to see his words as an attack on these manifestations of clergyhood wherever they occur: "Do not be called 'Rabbi.' You have but one teacher, and you are all brothers. Call no one on earth your father; you have but one Father in heaven. Do not be called 'Master'; you have but one master, the Messiah" (Matt 23:8-10). And in verse 5: "All their works are performed to be seen. They widen their phylacteries and lengthen their tassels."

This may be the place to note that the potentially noxious tendencies inherent in every clergyhood may have their effects not only in the individual cleric but in the collective psyche of the group. Particular members of a community become members of a clergy group, as we have said, by passing through its distinctive entrance portal. That takes the form of graduation from a university or the police academy, certification by a legal or medical authority, or priestly ordination. Those members do so individual by individual. And each one wears the group's habits (an interesting term in itself) in a quite individual fashion. That fact may cause us to overlook the *collective* identity of the group, the subtle and not so subtle colorations that begin to be imprinted on the individual members of the group, sometimes without them being aware of the way they are being shaped and identified. It is these colorations which make the clergy body a genuine culture.

Strengths can become weaknesses

We have noted the sense of identity that clergyhood confers on both the clergy and the laity in the particular system. It is a contribution to the ordered life of a community, a positive benefit that should not be underestimated. Having guilds of people with specialized skills gives everyone a sense of security. The presence of these guilds also frees up the energies of the rest of the community for other equally laudable pursuits. By virtue of differentiation of gifts and roles, society is able to tend to more complex needs. An amoeba may be a beautifully simple organism, but all it can do is amoeb. By recognizing special gifts in recognized subsets of the members, the community as a whole can achieve multiple goals. Amoebas can't make the exquisite contribution made by a diversified bee colony.

As is the case with so many other things, though, that very strong sense of identity can lead to effects which actually diminish the benefits created by the gathered empowerment of the whole. The strengths derived from clergy solidarity can become impediments, as members use the collective identity to distance themselves from the population they serve. In Philadelphia, one of the grand jurors in the clergy sexual abuse investigation there reflected on the behavior of Cardinal Bevilacqua. She wondered how it was possible to have such power and do nothing to stop the evils. She concluded that regardless of what the cardinal did, he knew he'd always have people supporting him.

Clerics are sensitive to critique

Every clergy body develops defenses to protect the benefits it is bringing to society. In the first instance that shows up as sensitivity to any form of critique of the body. This can be manifested in their relationship to outsiders who offer perceptions which might reveal that the clothes of the emperor or empress, if not totally lacking, are quite tattered and do not quite conceal blemishes in the picture. In the extreme case even constructive suggestions for improvement are resisted. The very notion that the laity might appropriately assess clergy performance is called into question. After all, "Who are they to dare to critique? Do they realize how hard it has been for us to master the unique competence that grounds our existence? Do they appreciate what it's like to oversee troops, or work in the emergency room, or do research in a musty law library or archive, or listen to the complaints of people who don't know the first thing about church history? What do they really *know*?"

It was noted with some irony that when Lawrence Summers had to step down as president of Harvard that the main opposition came from a body of college professors who themselves are quite impervious to critique from anyone outside their club.

Unexamined Attitude

Clergy: "We are special. Who are 'they' to judge us?"

Laity: "They are the experts. I'm sure they know what they're talking about."

This general sensitivity to critique leads to a reluctance on the part of members within the group to assume responsibility for critiquing the performance of others in the same guild. This reluctance can be a manifestation of unacknowledged self-protection. If I were to challenge my fellow lodge member, I could open myself up to embarrassing revelations of my own deficiencies. In the parlance of the street it's called "CYA": cover your abutment.

In a more crucial sense, though, the inability to employ internal criticism betrays a loss of understanding of the service that the creation of the clergy was meant to provide. It indicates a loss of focus on the mission of the clerical group, whether that be "societal health" or "justice" or "responsible scholarship" or "public safety"—

or "the search for the holy." Doctors are notoriously loath to blow the whistle on their colleagues for medical malpractice. In an address to healthcare professionals forty years ago, Abraham Heschel noted that the work of the practicing physician is seldom subject to public evaluation. The patient's reliance upon his doctor is often due to blind faith. The legal profession rarely chastises, much less disbars, unethical lawyers. Generals rarely pay the price for things like torture; that is visited upon the scapegoats, the grunts. The existence of the "blue line" by which police officers shield the bad guys in their profession is legendary. On the intellectual front, academics may throw spitballs at each other for sloppy scholarship, but that tends to be more a display of one-upmanship than a serious effort at academic integrity or accountability.

What then of the ordained? Our long Christian tradition holds up fraternal correction as an important component of discipleship within the community of faith, but its practice is far less in evidence than even the preaching about it, and that is rare indeed. As difficult as it is for the baptized in general to challenge a sister or brother in the faith, the strong loyalty inbred by clergification makes it doubly hard within the clerical club. One is reminded of the Eleventh Commandment of the Republican Party: "Thou shalt not criticize another Republican."

Unexamined Attitude

Clergy: "If you criticize our profession you are disrespecting us as persons. We do not allow outsiders (or insiders) to criticize anyone in our guild."

Laity: "We lack the credentials for judging them; we have to trust that they'll take care of that internally."

In the case of the ordained, the burden of group loyalty can become even more oppressive. To blow the whistle may require speaking out about the behavior of the one to whom a priest has vowed holy obedience, his bishop. And it is perhaps even more difficult for one of the most deeply vested members of the episcopal guild to critique the behavior of a fellow ordinary. It may call for a great reservoir of ego strength—or heroic character, if one prefers that rhetoric—to act out of one's basic sense of right and break through the facade of the sacred.

Clerics focus on image

The corporate rejection of critique frequently takes the form of saving the *image* of the body. Now reputation, to be sure, is an invaluable asset for an individual or a group. Protecting one's reputation is a natural and healthy response to unwelcome news. However, when guilds react defensively to protect their image, the phrase is actually quite precise: what becomes the target of the response is the outsiders' perceptions of the group rather than the truth of the critique. The focus is not on the substance of the critique, on the actual performance of service that was the foundation of the community's original recognition, but on the collective ego of the clergy body. The primary loyalty is to the protection of the institution's image rather than the well-being of those for whom the clergy group supposedly exists. Addressing the real issues raised by the critique is construed as disloyalty, especially by those who have been chosen guardians of the collective body: police chiefs, generals, deans, heads of medical associations, and bishops. (Or presidents for that matter.)

Unexamined Attitude

Clergy: "Protecting our image is more important than confronting the situation. If someone blows the whistle on us we will deflect the question and attack the messenger."

Laity: "People shouldn't say things that undermine the profession."

Once again, there is an irony here. The divide that separates a clergy from its corresponding laity, and the timidity engendered and accepted as their script by laypeople, can become so great that it frequently prevents the clergy from hearing how they really *are* perceived. Being shielded from the true assessments of the laity—one of the manifestations of that "losing touch with reality" mentioned earlier—leads the clergy to react to their self-created exaggerations of lay attitudes, rather than to the laity's actual appraisals. Except when the situation has deteriorated badly and trust has fundamentally eroded, laity are actually inclined to take an affirming stance toward the foibles of their clergy; they value the role of the clergy and will go to great lengths to protect them, because the presence of clergy helps them maintain a sense of security in a chaotic world. But how can the clergy appreciate that if they shut down the avenues for listening in the first place? If the fear of hearing anything negative controls your psyche, it anesthetizes your ability to appreciate the genuinely positive.

Unexamined Attitude

Clergy: "If we ignore what people are saying about us, we won't have to change anything."

Laity: "I'm sure they know how we feel; my saying something won't tell them anything they haven't already heard."

The power of arcane language

Another collective effect of a clerical culture is its creation of an arcane language. What began as a wisdom that could be comprehended by the laity they were called to serve morphs into a terminology accessible only to those in the inner circle.

Once again we must stress that this is a natural development as fields of special knowledge and expertise become more and more differentiated. Emerging disciplines generate special terminology because the questions they are exploring require constant refinement. The word "genome" was not even in our vocabulary fifty years ago. Its use today (for those in the know) compacts broad ranges of ideas into an easily usable shorthand, saving us from having to use exhaustive circumlocutions.

In the process, however, the laity can become seriously marginalized and disempowered, even in areas of great significance for their lives. Medical jargon can become a wall that shuts laypersons out and tells them they are incapable of understanding their own bodies. (We may forget that until recent times it was unthinkable that laypersons be allowed to see their own hospital chart.) Legal "whereases" have long been the stuff of satire, which would be entertaining if it didn't sometimes have disastrous consequences in the lives of real people (think insurance policies). In the case of academic jargon, even professors may be healthy enough to laugh at the titles of dissertations or articles occasioned by the publish-or-perish syndrome: "The intertextuality of metaphysical gossip in ninth-century Vanuatu" and the like. We can enjoy their absurdity because they cause no harm to the general public. However, when unnecessarily arcane language makes it into classrooms on a regular basis, it becomes a barrier to real learning for overwhelmed and confused students.

Unexamined Attitude

Clergy: "It takes special knowledge and training to become certified. The matters we deal with are beyond the comprehension of the laity."

Laity: "I don't understand what he's telling me, but that's why he's the doctor."

But the marginalizing of the lay public (a hazard incurred in every instance of clericalization) can have serious consequences. During the Vietnam era the point was well made in the form of the slogan: "War is too serious to leave to the generals." When the language of the inner circle is used effectively to take away from the laity decision making and adult responsibility for choices of great moments in their lives, serious mischief is afoot. The destructive impact is multiplied when the laity become complicit in their own disempowerment by allowing the situation to continue by default. Variations on the Vietnam slogan might include: "our health is too important to leave to the doctors"; "justice is too important to leave to the lawyers"; "an education is too important to leave to the professors"; and "the life of the spirit is too important to leave to the ordained."

Economic advancement confers status

The passage from lay status to clergyhood is frequently accompanied by economic advancement. Doctors, lawyers, and university professors ordinarily enjoy a living standard above that of the majority of people in society. Public safety practitioners and military officers, though not considered wealthy, are usually comfortable enough. The ordained, although they may not exactly embrace a preferential option for the poor, are for the most part the least financially compensated among professional groups. The relatively lower compensation of Catholic clergy does not mean personal finances are a nonfactor in assessing the impact of clergyhood on the ordained, however. In fact, the normal American practice is that ordained pastors in the Catholic community receive significant benefits, not in the form of salary but in the form of housing, food, and automobile allowance: the so-called "hidden" revenues. The fact that these are not normally accounted for in dollars can lead to a form of economic naiveté if not blindness. I experienced this once while facilitating the meeting of the priests of a diocese:

> We were teaching the priests a particular method for reaching consensus, and the subject happened to be their compensation. We had the group listing various assumptions they held, among which were several in the "pity-us" category. It was only after some time that my partner, a layman who the priests probably considered well-off (he was a consultant, after all) suddenly realized what they were talking about. He leaned over to me and said, "These guys aren't talking about living expenses, they're talking about walking-around money, discretionary income! I wish I had that much free cash after paying my mortgage and food and transportation bills . . ."

Here is another manifestation of the way clergyhood may subtly lead to a loss of touch with realities faced by the people in their pews.

Over the centuries, entry into the ordained clergy has been for many, if not the way out of economic insecurity, at least the stepping-stone to enhanced status. It is not unfair to suggest that such a motivation may be a contributing factor in the surge of vocations to the priesthood in the underdeveloped countries of our world today. It would take a suspiciously supernaturalized view of religious calling to ignore this reality. I once heard a fine American priest describe the genesis of his priestly vocation in these terms:

> We lived in a mill town, where it was a given that once you left high school you would spend your working life in the big manufacturing plant that anchored the economy of the town. One day I heard a visiting Passionist mission preacher. He was the most educated person I had ever met. I asked to go to the seminary. Looking back after forty years I can say without any shame that joining the community was my way out of the factory. That doesn't diminish in any way my vocation. God uses all sorts of motivations; we're not angels.

He was simply honest about the economic element in his call to ordination, a refreshing change from the disembodied, almost heretical, presentations in so much discussion of vocations.

Clerics lose touch with those to be served

Another result of the embodiments mentioned above can be that the clergy lose appreciation for the daily realities faced by the laity they are called to serve that are quite embodied indeed. In the medical arena, for example, schedules and transportation challenges can make it all but impossible for patients to get to medical appointments. Even the most sensitive and dedicated pastors may not fully appreciate what is involved in the lives of their parishioners.

The late Father Jim Provost, a distinguished canonist as well as much-loved pastor, made the point eloquently by way of a personal confession:

> I was the pastor of a parish in Butte, Montana. If you had asked me if I really understood my people I would have been indignant. Of

course I know my people! But a simple experience revealed to me that I was wrong. Some priest-friends from seminary days were taking a vacation trip and stopped to visit me for a couple of days. I was wondering how to entertain them. The Anaconda copper mine is a huge open pit right in the heart of the city, and one of the tourist attractions consists of an educational foray into "the hole." So I decided to treat my guests to that experience, although I had never taken the trip myself. We got into the elevator and within three minutes down in that shaft, even in the diluted form of a guided tour, I realized that I hadn't the foggiest idea of the experience of what my parishioners went through every day down in those bleak and grim caverns. After that day I could never preach to them in the same way.

Unexamined Attitude

Clergy: "We know what is important in the life of the laity; we don't have to experience it ourselves to give them advice on what to do about it."

Laity: "We can't expect them to understand all the demands on us; their profession makes them different from us."

Distinction turns into superiority

It should be evident that the presence of a particular gift in some but not all members of society does not make the gifted ones superior in nature to others. Gifts are just that: ultimately unmerited even if they have been further cultivated and enhanced by the labors of their bearers. They do not change the intrinsic worth of human personhood, which is already the supreme value in itself.

But when those gifts come to be recognized by society and, beyond that, are recognized as constituting a distinct identity for one group within the society, experience shows that it can require great maturity to retain focus on the inherent equality of all human persons. "Higher" and consequently "lower" forms of status tend to emerge, at times with damaging effect for everyone involved.[4]

---

4. In *The New American Militarism: How Americans are Seduced by War,* Andrew Bacevich observes the process at work in the military: "Noting with regret

And both share responsibility for the resulting situation, the clergy for resting on their privileges or even demanding the privileges they've been given, and the laity for accepting a demeaning definition of their self-worth.

Unexamined Attitude

Clergy: "Our calling and training makes us superior to the laity."

Laity: "Their profession makes them better than us."

If the tendency is not resisted, the reality can be harmful enough in the case of clergy such as physicians, lawyers, scholars, or those who care for our security. But in the case of the ordained clergy and religious laity, the effects are more profound because they touch upon the realm of the spirit. The gift which is then attributed to the ordained is that of unique access to the divine, to God. The ordained can buy into such an illusion and the laity maintain it. The result is that they both draw the conclusion that laity are second-class citizens in the realm of the spirit, that the One whom Jesus called Father is less near to them by virtue of their lay status. If that becomes the prevailing mindset, the harm to the community of faith is great indeed.

Unexamined Attitude

Clergy: "Simply by our vocation as ordained ministers we are specialists in the realm of the spirit, and the laity aren't."

Laity: "They're the pros in the things of God; we're just amateurs."

---

that 'the armed forces are no longer representative of the people they serve,' retired admiral Stanley Arthur has expressed concern that 'more and more, enlisted as well as officers are beginning to feel that they are special, better than the society they serve.' Such tendencies, concluded Arthur, are 'not healthy in the armed forces serving a democracy.'" (New York: Oxford University Press, 2005), 24.

Clericalism breeds secrecy and lack of accountability

As I have indicated, the results named here were in no particular order. They were just thrown out randomly. But no matter how they are ordered it seems safe to say that, taken cumulatively, they tend to generate one most significant effect. It is a form of separation that renders the clerical group fundamentally unaccountable to any outside power that might shield it from its own worst faults. Clergy groups develop a secret world that is quite impenetrable. Transparency is not come by easily, even when what might be concealed are clearly criminal acts. The separation involved in clergyhood can make the clergy act as if they are not subject to the laws that the rest of society is obliged to respect. They can lose a sense of citizenship and solidarity with the laity.

Unexamined Attitude

Clergy: "We don't have to be accountable to the laity. We are their shepherds."

Laity: "What would we do without our priests?"

Two embarrassing illustrations from real life may make the point. Sadly, they both happen to involve bishops:

> A new bishop had been appointed to a diocese. A community of male religious who conducted a school there wanted to offer welcome and hospitality to the new ordinary. He was invited to a dinner with the community. After pleasantries over drinks a small group invited the bishop to join them at table for the dinner itself. One of the men asked the bishop if he'd care for a glass of wine. He accepted the offer but upon taking a first sip he said, "Who the hell bought this crap!"

Regardless of his ordination and church position, the man deserves no respect because he has no respect for others.

> Another ordinary of a large archdiocese called in the layman who served as the diocesan business manager. Without any discussion, the ordinary told him of his plan to renovate a vacation house for

himself and some priests. The business manager was instructed to move $1,000,000 from the diocesan account to the bishop's discretionary fund. The manager spontaneously replied, "I can't just do that, bishop. We haven't budgeted for it and it's the people's money." To which the archbishop said simply, "Well, from now on it's my money."

When a member of the episcopacy becomes as estranged from solidarity with the people as these two were, who holds them accountable?

As for accountability within the group itself, we have noted already the reluctance of clergy to critique anyone within the circle of the group. Among the ordained Catholic clergy, there are no organizational structures designed to enhance the performance of the ordinary priest, much less a diocesan bishop. A priest friend who had been a civil lawyer before he entered the seminary told me of an amazing realization that came to him upon his ordination and entry into pastoral ministry. He was amazed to discover that except for something like blatant heresy, there was no medium to hold him accountable for anything. Surgeons and lawyers need insurance against malpractice suits. A pastor can blithely preach blatant nonsense for years with no one to call him to account.

I recall hearing a priest giving a homily to a vacation crowd at the Jersey shore; he was inveighing against birth control and observed that in his dealings with high school students he had never met anyone from a large family who had emotional problems. Where does the laity turn for recourse in the face of such idiocy?

As a tragic illustration of what such a freewheeling clubbiness can lead to, consider another real-life example:

> The bishop was the ordinary of a large diocese on the edge of a major metropolitan area. The diocese was populated by many highly educated, professional people. They often commented that the bishop was invisible. He was simply a non-presence in the local church. That fact is not too hard to understand when one learns that it was common knowledge that he spent every Sunday morning playing golf at the most prestigious country club in the area.

How out of touch with the reality of one's calling could you be? The same bishop could call a priest on the carpet for some trivial variation in liturgical choreography or expression, yet there was no recourse for the laity who suffered because of his own egregious selfishness.

The name itself creates the power

We have explored some of the embodiments of clergyhood, the contribution they make to societal health, and the tendency inherent within them to deteriorate into destructive pathologies. But when one analyzes the power they possess, it turns out that it ultimately resides in the name itself.

As a biblical people, we have been schooled to relate power and names. We understand, for example, the transfer of power that takes place when God renames Abram, or when Jesus calls Simon Peter "Rock." We know that the name bespeaks a conferral of power. It is important for us to get beneath the external manifestations to the names themselves, to reflect on the rich implications of the names we confer. Genuine power accrues to the individuals in a corporate enterprise through the names we give them.

How can that be? Because corporate endeavors acquire the power to affect people through networks of human communication. In those networks the group's name is crucial. Say "IBM" and a whole host of responses are inevitably evoked in people (as is easily seen if, instead of IBM, you were to say "the XYZ Corporation"). A group's name has all the power of an icon, because it sums up and holds within itself all the actions of the present members as well as those of their predecessors, as perceived by the surrounding society. Think "France," for example. A culture's name is like an atom into which a whole host of energies has been bundled, or a diamond that is capable of so many hues because of a solidifying process that took place over centuries.

To use a personal illustration: When I am asked to identify myself, I respond that I am a Jesuit. An extraordinary thing happens. Consciously or unconsciously, and depending on the person's range of experience with Jesuits, I can be seen as one with a whole host of enormously significant persons, known and unknown. In the psyche of the people I am meeting, I may be associated with a Francis Xavier or a Peter Canisius; perhaps more immediately with a John Courtney Murray or Pedro Arrupe. I may benefit from the aura of some confessor or spiritual director who accompanied one of these people through a life-transforming conversion. Or perhaps I enjoy the borrowed glory of a teacher who saw potential in one of them and patiently enabled the young woman to believe in her gifts or the young man to put his pain at the service of someone else.

As an individual I am empowered by all these preconscious associations. The gifts, the accomplishments, the commitment, and zeal of these brothers of mine accrue to me. They become social capital. The name introduces me into this new setting, not as some lonely, autonomous individual having to break into the situation on my own, but as a bearer of a heritage, a culture. The corporate history shaped by all these men is present with me as soon as the word "Jesuit" is spoken—not unlike what happens with words like "Franciscan" or "Benedictine" or "Dominican" or "Lutheran." All that bundled energy I mentioned earlier is present and active in the interchange.

I may not personally know the individuals whose lives and deeds are creating this space for me. I may not even recognize the names mentioned. Their life in the Society of Jesus may have ended long before mine began. I have never lived under the same roof with most of these men who lend power to my impact. I would be less than honest if I did not add that I am also, as a result of this association, identified with men with whom I would probably disagree violently on all sorts of issues. I am lumped with men whose basic ideologies are inimical to my vision of what God is about in our world, and with oddballs, cranks, and assorted neurotics whose certifiability depends only on who does the certifying.

The point is that through this mysterious process I, the individual, am more than myself. Those persons or groups who meet me under the designation "Jesuit" (or, as the experience is broadened, "Ignatian") are predisposed. They are ready to grant me a hearing, an initial acceptance, a chance, some sort of new possibility of making an impact in their world. The name not only gives access to power; it is power.

This latter reflection brings us to a core insight. Clergyhoods are about power. They are not simply communities or juxtapositions of even very gifted individuals. By bringing these individuals together under a common name, the qualities and characteristics of those who have worn that ancient name coalesce and have a new kind of impact on the people from whom they have been drawn.

In the Ignatian view, power is a creature. In itself it is neutral. It can function for good or evil. The original analog for power is physical: material energy. We would be unable to accomplish much in this world were all the rivers to dry up, the winds to cease to blow, or if the energies locked up in seams of coal or fields of oil or gas were rendered inaccessible to us. Yet each of those forms of power can run amok and destroy whole civilizations.

And so our question is now more clearly focused. What determines whether a particular form of clergyhood unleashes the benefits to society which were anticipated at its creation? Or, conversely, when does it become a destructive force that diminishes the gifts of those who become laity when it arrives on the human stage?

The answer depends on whether the individuals who are invited to share in the empowerment brought by clergyhood can remain true to the original challenge implied in their calling to serve their corresponding laity. It is only that commitment which can hold at bay its destructive potential. For physicians, it requires placing the healing of people above all self-interest. For academics, it must mean the unyielding pursuit of the truth no matter where that leads. For lawyers, it is a fierce commitment to the work of building a just society. Peacekeepers must pursue every measure that gives hope of reaching nonviolent resolution of inevitable human conflict.

And for the ordained? The members of that clergy are called to live out, within the service they provide to the community of the faithful, the same call to priesthood that challenges every last member of the laity.

We have arrived at that other reality we are trying to untangle from its confusion with clergyhood, the religious reality: engagement with the divine. We turn now to priesting.

Chapter Two
Priesting Before Clergyhood

We have seen that clergyhood is not limited to those we customarily call priests. And we have outlined some of the features that characterize clergyhood, whether that of the physicians, the lawyers, the academics, the military, or the ordained. One way to avoid the unexamined attitudes that result in a clerical culture is to focus on the call to be clergy. Why does society set apart a particular clergy? In the case of the ordained, what is desired is priesting. However, that term refers to a more complicated reality than we have been using it to describe. It turns out that before there was an ordained clergy, there was a priesthood already in place, one that we need to reclaim today. We turn first to the evidence from the early church, the New Testament.

New Testament Evidence

Perhaps the first thing that might surprise a general audience (though it is commonplace among biblical scholars) is the fact that the writers in the New Testament never refer to any single individual as a "priest"—except for the person of Christ himself. The New Testament does indeed refer to a *priesthood.* But it is clear from the context that the reference is to the whole community of the baptized: "you are 'a chosen race, a royal priesthood, a holy nation, a people of his own, so that you may announce the praises' of him who called you out of darkness into his wonderful light. Once you were 'no people' but now you are God's people;

you 'had not received mercy,' but now you have received mercy" (1 Pet 2:9-10). Baptism is the threshold across which one passes into the priesthood made up of the body of the faithful.

The church of that era did of course single out particular individuals who possessed unique gifts and were challenged to use those gifts for the building up of the community. Passages like 1 Corinthians 12:28 and Ephesians 4:11 present lists of such gifted individuals. We read of "apostles," "teachers," "pastors," "evangelists," and so forth—but not of priests. The lists contain roles which would scarcely figure in any attempt to portray the ordinary structures of our contemporary church. No present-day parish bulletin I know of would list the community's evangelists or healers, for example. And yet the scriptural texts do not include the one role that most ordinary people would place high on the list of descriptors of today's church. They do not say "and some are priests." The community assemblies, whether eucharistic or not, would have had leaders, to be sure. But at that early stage they were not yet called priests, much less set apart from people called laity in the fashion of today's clergy.

The Scriptures do make reference to men called "presbyters." The term refers to elders of some sort. But to interpret the text in such a way as to identify these men as what we would call today "priests" is surely misguided. In a wholly unwarranted fashion it projects back into the text present-day ecclesiastical realities. Such a mode of interpretation seems to be an effort to avoid an awkward and disturbing challenge that is clearly posed by the actual texts: a church with no priests?

A more intellectually honest approach is available. Suppose we were to take the texts at face value. We would acknowledge what seems to be the plain fact. The early Christian communities knew no distinction among their members that would remotely correspond to our contemporary understanding of the difference between ordained priests and the laity. It would have been simply too early in their development as human communities. Organizational development does not work like that. Role differentiation involves a gradual evolution, even for an institution whose focus is on the transcendent.

Many scholars take the data at face value and put their energies into trying to understand *why* no member of the community was called priest. One common conjecture is that it was because the New Testament writers would have wanted to avoid any confusion with the simultaneous reality of pagan priests, practitioners of mystery cults. Such pagan priests were a significant part of the context within which the early communities of Jesus' followers were trying to understand the new religious identity they were experiencing. In the linguistic context of that day, to call a church leader "priest" would have brought with it a whole host of associations that the original small communities of Jesus' followers wanted precisely to get away from.

That is not an unreasonable conjecture. But another explanation for the omission may be equally plausible and perhaps more persuasive.

An Organizational Development Perspective

In the past fifty years, through the discipline of organizational development, we have made significant strides in understanding the stages through which communities pass in the process of differentiation among their members. Applying those insights, it would not be difficult to imagine how the gifts enumerated in the Scriptures came to enjoy institutional recognition in the early communities. An early member of the church at Corinth might have said to her neighbor, "Have you noticed how good Phoebe is at interpreting what people are trying to say when they begin speaking in tongues? We need to listen to her." Or, "Silas is so persuasive when he tells outsiders why the Gospel impels us to care for one another. When I meet people inquiring about us, I send them directly to him." Others would have noted and acknowledged these gifted people and the community would have begun to call on their gifts on a more routine basis. It is perfectly normal for more regularized roles to begin to emerge as the life of a small community of disciples unfolds. More abstract titles are soon crafted to capsulize the behaviors of these people who have now become community agents. The reflection makes the question "Why aren't any called priests?" all the more pressing.

The more cogent reason why the communities did not refer to individual priests would appear to be simply that another notion enjoyed far more power in the self-understanding of these early disciples. It is the concept latent in the term the Scripture writers actually did use: we, *the whole community*, are the "holy priesthood," the replacement for the priests of the Old Covenant. A similar notion is expressed in the letter to the Hebrews. In that case it is about the teaching role. "And they shall not teach, each one his fellow citizen / and kinsman, saying, 'Know the Lord,' / for *all* shall know me, / from least to greatest" (8:11; emphasis added). We might easily draw the conclusion that any distinction within the early communities that might risk diminishing the primal sense that all are peers in the pilgrimage of holiness was to be avoided. To designate any individual member a priest in a way that distinguishes him from the other members of the holy community or, much less, elevates him above them (which, as we have seen, is one tendency that comes with every clergyhood) distorts the nature of the Gospel message.

The "royal priesthood" portrayed in Scripture has, of course, been interpreted as something merely metaphorical over against the *real* priesthood embodied by the ordained. As a mere figure of speech it is then easily dismissed as a pious abstraction. Those who are not ordained are relegated to some second-class kind of holiness. "Father" has a direct line to God (a comment every priest has heard all too often), and he becomes the medium through which the non-ordained gain access to the divine. (No one puts the matter that baldly, but if you listen to the language of many laypeople, that is the message they heard. It is one of their unexamined attitudes. As Scholastic philosophy wisely taught us: communication happens not in the intention of the sender but in the mind of the receiver.)

One might argue from the actual Scripture text that the understanding of the early community of Jesus' followers was that the collective body of believers is the real priesthood. The literal sense is the primary one. The later organizational subset of the ordained is the secondary or derivative use of the term. That does not make the ordained priesthood *merely* metaphorical, however. The priesthood of the ordained is real and not simply metaphorical. But it is meaningful only to the extent that it actually participates in and contributes to the life and holiness of the primary priesthood, the gathered faithful.

At this point it might be wise to confront head-on the question raised by a good theologian friend upon reading the first draft of this work: "Does this position deny that there is an essential distinction between the priesthood of the baptized and that of the ordained?" The answer is no, it does not. It takes no position on such a question. Our concern is to understand the process by which the useful metal of clergification is debased and transformed into the dross of clericalism (a distinction we will explore more fully in chapter 3). It is a question of how the church really works. In the world of social dynamics, the language of essential or accidental distinctions serves no purpose. People just don't live in that kind of a mental world. But they are affected, deeply, by the behaviors they experience.

The Substantive Content of Priesting

If priesthood precedes clergification (and the laicization that goes with it), what are its features? As a reality and not a mere metaphor, priesthood must manifest itself in attitudes and behavior. How is priesthood—as contrasted from, not opposed to, clergyhood—embodied? When does priestly identity come to expression?

First consider the accepted usage of the word "priest," a man in holy orders. Under that usage the image of the priest as the cultic and community leader of a body of the faithful provides us with clear and accepted indices, ways by which priesthood is embodied. We know what "priest" means, what laity reasonably expects of such a man. Modern churchgoing Catholics reveal their actual criteria for priesthood in the questions they ask when they meet a priest for the first time: "Where do you *say Mass*, Father? Where's your *parish*?" I have been welcomed with these questions many times. A clericalized understanding of contemporary priesthood is further revealed when a priest happens to be in lay dress when he is first introduced to a layperson: "Oh, I didn't realize you were a priest, Father; sorry . . ."

Suppose we were not to begin from our accustomed (and clericalized) view of a priest, however. Suppose, instead, that we adopt a New Testament view and focus on the ways in which priesthood is exercised by the broad body of believers. That body includes those who are ordained, though not as a distinct order, within the holy community. All simply and without distinction are called to act out of a priestly identity. The signs, the embodiments that are expected to flow from priestly identity, then, take on a different character. Being priest—acting priestly—is not a matter of liturgical presiding or being a canonically designated leader within the church community. Much less is it a matter of special clothing or address. It calls, rather, for actions flowing from a conversion, a new orientation in the soul brought about by the Spirit of Jesus.

Priestly behavior in that sense originates and culminates in an attitude of adoration, of humble presence before the all-holy One in the midst of a community of fellow worshipers. At the most profound level, that occurs in those special rituals by which the community participates in the life of the risen Jesus, in the liturgy. But for the most part the evidence—the actual priesting, if you will—shows up in the everyday life of people of faith. The standards for discovering its presence are found in the Beatitudes and the type of deeds highlighted in Matthew 25. The Christian community priests when its members take on the mind and heart of Jesus; when they show forth singleness of purpose in their following of the risen Lord; when their daily lives are an expression of praise and gratitude—and joyous song—to the One Jesus called "Father"; when they identify compassionately with the broken and dispossessed of society; when they relate personally to others as peers, as brothers and sisters; and when they use the power of their voice to speak out and act for the rights of the voiceless. More simply, the community priests when they love the Lord with their whole heart and their whole mind and their whole soul, and their neighbor, and even their enemy, as themselves. We must be wary of reducing to a stale cliché the profound truth of the ancient saying by which an amazed pagan world described the attraction of the Christian community: "See how these Christians love one another."[1]

This priesthood of the believing community translates into a call for ceaseless pilgrimage, an intense search for the most genuine, present response to the transcendent, holy One who loved us first and reveals the Way in the life, death, and resurrection of Jesus. Because it is a pilgrimage, such a life is ever underway, never completed or settled. Priests are in a continuous, costly process of conversion. The expressions of priesting in any cultural context are always subject to challenge and criticism, because they never fully match and satisfy the impulse out of which they emerge. That priesthood calls for a *radical confrontation with reality* in the pursuit of truth. Truth about the self of the holy community and truth about the individual within it, in light of the Truth who is the God ever creating it. It involves continual presence to what *is,* including both its beauty and its ugly sinfulness. As difficult as such a commitment is to live out, avoidance of reality and our shared responsibility for it is not an option. The organizational guru Peter Drucker, someone not usually associated with religion, once described saints as those who see reality. And the reality is that the God who *is* creates and confronts us at every present moment. The further reality is that, though that confrontation takes the form of the Lord's infinite compassion, it does not reduce us to passive non-responsibility. The God who creates also labors within us. And the creative labor of the Holy One consists precisely in making us free agents who share responsibility for the unfolding of the single drama of the universe, the locus in which that mysterious reality called the kingdom of God comes.

To put it succinctly: clergyhood involves playing a role expected by society; it is a *state.* Priesting is a way of living, a *life.* Like any

1. Tertullian, *Apologeticus,* ch. 39.

form of life it is not a state but a process unfolding through appropriate action. It is never achieved but always being actuated in the present moment, or else it is in danger of atrophying. If we stop breathing—physically or spiritually—we die.

Role and Performance

Roles are expressions of stratified social expectations. When people hear that a man or woman is an ordained minister, a whole host of customary or stereotypical expectations are evoked. Society looks to things like leadership of a worshiping community ("What *parish* do you serve, Father?"). It expects the person to be more or less familiar with or fluent in the holy texts of the community: to help others to understand them and to be able to challenge a community with the demands that flow from them. It recognizes the person's status through external forms: title, dress, perhaps distinctive residential site. ("Where's your rectory/parsonage/vicarage, Pastor?") It assesses the person's performance (a word taken from drama, after all) on the basis of criteria accepted and made normative by way of custom over the years.

"He's a decent enough preacher." "She has a good way of pastoring the sick and homebound." "A nice enough fellow, but he sure runs lousy meetings." "Totally unorganized." "Tracks the funds of the parish like a hawk." "He's a glad-hander," or "a cold fish."

When people reveal in offhand remarks the kind of criteria they are actually using to evaluate their shepherds, the accent usually falls on a clergy role at which the ordained person proves adept or inept. Of course the hope that he or she might *also* be living the Gospel message of Jesus is there in some fashion, but it is more of an aura or atmospheric. It functions as a vague backdrop behind the more consciously named forms of service the community is asking of its minister. The priesting of an ordained minister—the pilgrimage of holiness incumbent on the occupier of the role by virtue of the baptismal call shared with everyone else in the community—is treated more as a personal or even private matter.

Whether the minister is holy is his business, or hers. A nice extra but not part of the job expectation. And beyond that, the fact that this ordained person is a *sinner,* although it is never explicitly denied by the community, is rarely held in the forefront of their consciousness. For some in the community, if they were ever to allow the sinfulness of their pastor even the minimum space on their screen, their frightened and tenuous hold on the sacredness of their church would be thrown into jeopardy.

The late Monsignor Bob Fox of the South Bronx once mused to me about the participation of the ordained clergy in the penitential rite at the beginning of Mass: "Here's the leader of the holy community confessing that he is a grievous sinner! You'd think the people would be shocked at the idea. But of course they aren't—because they know he's just saying it but doesn't really mean it . . ."

It's not the congregation's fault; it's the way they were catechized by a clericalized church (regardless of whether their catechists were ordained or lay). To confront the fact that the minister is on the same clouded journey, however, would be too scary, because it makes the laity more responsible. They would no longer be able to project responsibility onto a guaranteed icon. In reality, both the ordained and the laity are called to radical holiness and personal responsibility by their common baptism. And in reality, all fall short.

A Foundation of Priesthood

Long before ordination, those who are merely baptized and not yet clergified are already members of the priesthood, called by virtue of their baptism to a life of radical holiness, without grade or distinction.

It is hard to overstate the extraordinary step in magisterial teaching on this point that was taken by the Second Vatican Council. In the fifth chapter of *Lumen Gentium*, the Dogmatic Constitution on the Church, the council fathers taught for the first time in such a definitive fashion that all members of the church are called to the fullness of holiness:

Christ . . . loved the church as his Bride, giving himself up for it so as to sanctify it (see Eph 5:25-26); he joined it to himself as his body and endowed it with the gift of his holy Spirit for the glory of God. Therefore, all in the church, whether they belong to the hierarchy or are cared for by it, are called to holiness, according to the apostle's saying: "For this is the will of God, your sanctification" (1 Thess 4:3; see Eph 1:4). This holiness of the church is shown constantly in the fruits of grace which the Spirit produces in the faithful and so it must be; it is expressed in many ways by the individuals who, each in their own state of life, tend to the perfection of charity, and are thus a source of edification for others. . . . It is therefore quite clear that all Christians *in whatever state or walk in life* are called to the fullness of Christian life and to the perfection of charity, and this holiness is conducive to a more human way of living even in society here on earth. (*LG,* par. 39 and 40, emphasis added.)

At least two serious implications flow from this dramatic pronouncement. The first is that any form of language which implies or suggests a higher form of holiness to be imputed to the ordained (with its implied corollary of a lower set of expectations for the laity) must be strenuously resisted as counter to the teaching of the church. Those who are called to orders are not thereby holier than their lay brothers and sisters. It is not then belittling of their dignity to say that nothing more is expected of them by way of Christian virtue or life than of the laity, *because the call to the fullness of perfection was already given in their baptism.*

The second corollary should be obvious. The call to the fullness of holiness does not cease upon entrance to the clerical state. Ordination is not graduation from the call to holiness. When they are ordained and become distinguished from the lay membership of the church, ministers are still subject to the radical Gospel call of love. They continue to be called to priesting. If not any more than the laity, also not less.

Holiness Based on Relationship

In a sense, the notion of priesting might be summed up by saying simply that it involves living the Gospel, which turns out to be anything but "simple." That Gospel call means acknowledging the fact that I have been and still am being created out of pure love by a God whose love always precedes any action on my part to earn that love. It means depending on the baptismal gift of the Spirit, poured into me by the saving love of the Son, to generate in me a fitting response to divine love. It means responding to God by loving in turn the creation which reflects the divine, and especially within that creation, my neighbor. It means that the love of my neighbor involves not only direct deeds of personal caring but also the ceaseless effort to transform, by whatever measure is given to me, all the unjust social structures which deprive my neighbor of the means to a life worthy of human dignity. But if we are to appreciate fully the distinctive harm caused by the clerical culture when its destructive potential is not resisted by one of its members, we need to highlight one profound element of the call to baptismal priesting: the challenge always to act *relationally* toward my neighbor.

My neighbor is a person, a singular embodiment of God's creation. A subject exactly like me. A free agent acting out the mystery of personhood, never merely the function of my need. I am called to awe and reverence and respect, to remove my sandals before the divine revealed in this person called neighbor, sister, brother. We are called to stand and relate free subject to free subject—face-to-face—and I am called to make my contribution to that relationship by being present to my partner. Personal relationship is peer-to-peer, inimical to any and all manifestations of superiority-inferiority, whatever their supposed ground.

The call to relate to the other as a person is a demanding discipline. It requires staying open to the other in the uniqueness of this present moment, no matter how the other responds or fails to respond to me. It involves transcendence of my ego—a form of death—in the interest of union with the other.

The reason this is so pertinent to our reflection on cleric*alism* is that one of the chief manifestations of that pernicious reality— perhaps its most destructive—is the objectification of persons. To the extent that we allow a role to dominate the interaction with another, to make of the other an inferior (or superior), the dignity of personhood and relationship is destroyed. Clergyhood and corresponding laicization are, as we have said, social roles. And as necessary and valuable as roles are in constructing a viable society, they bring with them the risk of depersonalization and objectification. The roles could be doctor-patient, professor-student, lawyer-client, officer-citizen, or pastor-sheep. They could be parent-child. In every case the role can be allowed to become so powerful that any sense of equal dignity—shared priesthood—is destroyed. People mutually create superiority-inferiority and abuse occurs. Not necessarily physical abuse but abuse nonetheless.

It is not easy to act always out of our priestly identity, to resist every temptation to superior-inferior interactions. Whether we acknowledge the tendency or not, as part of our reality as sinners all of us are inclined to find ways to participate in one-upmanship, whether as lord or as vassal. The basis might be possession of greater economic resources. It could be accumulation of knowledge, or sheer physical size, or even the ability to hit a ball with a bat. That general propensity is compounded when someone, beyond being simply neighbor, is called to a role of social responsibility vis-à-vis another person. Parenthood, for example, can degenerate into abuse of the personhood of a child without involving physical violence. It is the main thrust of this work that membership in a recognized clerical fraternity, with the enhancement of collective power, adds significantly to the risk of abusive behavior, actively perpetrated or passively accepted, to which all of us are subject as garden-variety human beings.

If that is so, our next question comes into focus, with respect to the ordained clergy in particular. What kinds of changes do occur when someone moves from being a member of the lay faithful to becoming a member of the ordained clergy? If the ordained are not expected to be *personally more holy* than those who are not ordained, what are we to expect of them? That is the subject of our next chapter.

Chapter Three

When Priests Become Ordained Clergy

It should be clear by now that when I use the word "priest" in the title of this chapter I am no longer using it in the customary sense of the ordained. We are building on the reflections on priesthood in chapter 2, so we can perhaps now take the risk of moving away from the traditional (but misplaced) language of "priests and laypeople" and begin speaking of individuals within the priesthood of the faithful, the baptized, simply as priests. Our question now becomes: what happens when such a baptized person, already priest, becomes a cleric?

Ordination: To What?

If people are priests already, prior to ordination, what does ordination do? Does it add something? Change something in the person? Or what? Let me begin by sharing a personal experience as our introduction to these questions:

> When I entered the Jesuits the course of formation leading to ordination was a thirteen-year program. We were being formed— molded into the Jesuit approach to life—by any number of spiritual role models. Some were canonical superiors, charged with leading a community of Jesuits more deeply into the Ignatian way of proceeding. Some were spiritual fathers, charged with attending to the inner life of individuals through regular one-on-one sharing and guidance in matters spiritual. Some were retreat directors,

attending to the work of the Spirit in times of more intense prayer for deeper conversion.

The message remained constant regardless of the one transmitting it: "Don't expect ordination to change you. Either you are a man of prayer and service to others now or you aren't. The one sure thing is that ordination won't make you become what you haven't already become when you arrive at that day." Regardless of the theological emphasis of the formation process—Pelagian can-do, dour Jansenist asceticism, or Ignatian discernment of spirits—the point was that you'd better be working at the conversion or priesting process all along the way. Ordination is not some magic act that will make you holy in an instant.

Then we entered upon a most significant moment: the final retreat before ordination. For me that event took place at the venerable Woodstock College. And more importantly, the retreat was directed by a most significant figure, Father John Courtney Murray. A renowned systematic theologian, destined three years later to become one of the *periti,* or special experts, at the Second Vatican Council, Murray was someone to be listened to with attention.

For thirteen years we had heard the mantra that "ordination won't change you; it won't make you what your own spiritual efforts in response to the guidance of the Holy Spirit haven't produced." You can imagine, then, the dislocation and confusion when this magisterial figure began the eight days by saying, "Ordination is going to change you, dramatically!"

I was faced with two sharply diverging positions. Ordination won't change you. Or, ordination will change you, and dramatically. Which is right? What does ordination change? And what doesn't it change?

Two Different Orders

My perplexity at the apparent contradiction between these two different answers continued for years. Actually, both are correct. Puzzlement finally yielded to resolution when I came to realize that the two positions were not really contradictory; they applied to two different orders of reality. The insight became the major premise of all the reflections in this book.

The earlier spiritual guides, in accord with a long tradition in the field of spiritual direction, were talking about the potential effect of ordination on the personal spiritual growth of the one being ordained. They were attempting to steer potential candidates away from an illusion: "No matter how I may have failed to cultivate a spiritual life during these years of formation, I will finally become holy when the bishop lays hands on me." Although they spoke in the language of personal spiritual growth rather than systematic theology, their admonition was rooted in a solid understanding of the nature of sacramental action. Sacraments are not magic. Although their ultimate efficacy comes from the action of the Holy Spirit, in the case of an adult the effectiveness of that action depends on the personal disposition of the one who receives the offer of grace. In that sense ordination does not make up for human irresponsibility by suddenly making someone personally holy. The one who is lazy or uncaring or self-centered on the day before ordination will be equally so on the day after.

Murray, on the other hand, was referring to a different, though no less consequential, order of reality. He was talking about the change that ordination necessarily brings in one's relation to the church, to the community of the faithful. He was alluding to the change in mutual expectations between the one being ordained, the rest of the clergy, and the lay members of the Lord's household. That is a matter of changed relationship and the changed expectations that flow from it, not enhancement of one's personal sanctity. As I pointed out in chapter 1, clergy are automatically associated with others in their profession. They receive some status whether they've proved themselves yet or not.

If it is an illusion to look for a change in one's interior spiritual life as a direct result of ordination, it is equally illusory to think that entry into the clerical state will *not* change one. Changes in relationships, and the new expectations they create, happen quite apart from the subjective state of the newly ordained. When new expectations (a new social order) are created through public status, one has no choice about *whether* to be changed. In the case of ordination that means the newly ordained is changed. So is the clergy group he or she becomes identified with. And so are the laity who now look to the newly ordained with new eyes and different hopes and expectations. In the social sphere of changed relationships, the choice is not whether one will be changed, but how one will choose to respond to the new order that has been created. By ordination a priest enters into membership in a group, the clergy, that is different from the priesthood to which the person was already (and remains) called by baptism. And that brings us to a new question and a new term.

Clergified or Clericalized?

Throughout the treatment of clergyhood in chapter 1 we stressed on repeated occasions that the creation of a clergy status, a clergyhood, can be a positive development for any society. On the other hand, it was also noted that every clergyhood brings with it the potential for effects which are destructive of healthy human community. To use the formulation of Pope John Paul II from the epigraph to this book: "Since culture is a human creation [it] is therefore marked by sin."

Here we might profitably introduce another set of terms. When one becomes a member of a clerical group we might say that he or she has been *clergified.* The term is intended in a quite neutral sense. It expresses the simple fact of inclusion in the class, with no connotation of value. The person passed board exams, the bar, made rank, or was ordained. The person has simply become a member of the clergy, with all the effects that such a membership brings, including the potential for the positive as well as for the negative.

What happens, on the other hand, when the person not only becomes included in the group but actually succumbs to those pernicious tendencies which have a way of accompanying any clergyhood? For this very different reality we might profitably say the person has become *clericalized.* (The term has the added advantage of sounding closer to the basic phenomenon we are trying to understand: clerica*lism*. That represents a general state of affairs in which the worst potentialities of clergyhood have been allowed to flourish and the clerical group as a whole has become oppressive of its corresponding laity.) An ordained minister who has allowed himself or herself to become clericalized has taken the low road and exhibits all the worst characteristics of a debased clergyhood. There is a loss of touch with the original call to service that grounded the creation of the clergy. It is replaced by a reliance on external forms such as dress, title, and perks. Some or all of the assumptions listed as occupational hazards of any clergy in chapter 1 are allowed to become the habitual mindset of the minister. Hypersensitivity to critique of one's performance; focus on external image in place of personal integrity and service; assumed self-importance accompanied by denigration and marginalization of the laity; secrecy and nonaccountability; attitudes of superiority—any or all are in evidence.

From what has been said, it should be clear that the risk that clergyhood will degenerate into clericalism is not limited to only the ordained. Nor is it gender-specific. It is present wherever members of any clergy in society unwittingly avoid shouldering the demanding responsibility for their own personal growth and integrity by overidentifying with a group that promises pre-packaged glory.

Clericalization of the Ordained

This distinction between clergification and clericalization—between benign and malignant clergyhood, if you will—carries with it unique consequences in the case of the ordained as contrasted with other forms of clergyhood. That is not to say the destruction is greater in the case of the ordained (abuse of personhood is an absolute evil in any case), but simply to note the unique character of its effects. When lawyers or physicians or academics or public security officials hide behind their role and act in a personally demeaning fashion toward their respective laity, they can inflict profound damage on the person's sense of self-worth and trust in the possibility of basic justice. In the case of the ordained clergy, when clericalization is allowed to flourish (and remember that both the clerics and the laity contribute to the process), the impact can be devastating not only for the individual's faith journey, but also for the whole faith community and the mission it proclaims to the broader society.

Concelebration and Priestly Support Groups: Unintended Consequences?

There is a certain irony to be noted in some developments in the theology and practice of the ordained since Vatican II. That council, in reaction to the individualized understanding and spirituality of priestly ordination prevalent at the time, placed a renewed stress on the corporate character of the Catholic priesthood. One way the restored vision was to be evidenced, for example, was in the reintroduction of the ancient practice of eucharistic concelebration. Several, or even very many, presbyters would act as a single body in visibly leading the community in worship. What better way to teach that ordination is not a personal gift of the individual presbyter, but rather entry into a single spiritual service exercised by a corporate body of specially certified and empowered men?

It may reasonably be argued that the practice has produced some salutary effects. On more solemn occasions the practice of concelebration, as an embodied expression, doubtless reminds those participating in it of the corporate nature of the ordained ministry more than any abstract treatise could.

But one may reasonably ask whether this call for a shift of vision, as happens with any such significant change in policy, has not also, in at least some instances, brought with it other consequences that are less-than-fully salutary. Consider this example:

> A partner and I were asked to facilitate a gathering of the bishops of a church region and the major superiors of male and female religious serving in that area. In the morning sessions the bishops and superiors were randomly assigned to table groups so that each

table would contain a proportional mix of bishops and superiors, men and women. The exchange at the tables was designed to promote peer relationships. No one, regardless of his or her status, had the answer. All were equals, and from the tone of the discussion it was clear that the participants enjoyed the experience of removing all distinction of status and entering into the give-and-take freely. The sharing was rich and valued by the participants.

Shortly before lunch the group was called to gather for Eucharist. The resulting situation within the community came as a shock. The sisters and several of the priests knelt or sat quietly in prayer in the body of the church. Then the concelebrants emerged: a phalanx of bishops all wearing their red zuchettas, plus some of the priests in full vestments. The disconnect from the experience of the morning could not have been more disconcerting.

Is this not an example of clericalization? The bishops and presbyters weren't required to concelebrate. Nothing in the occasion called for it. Indeed, some of the priests chose to participate from within the body of the faithful in the pews. In fact, the whole experience ran counter to what had been embodied in the preceding three hours. There was no educational purpose at stake; all of those present were quite aware of the corporate nature of the presbyterate and episcopate and needed no reminder. The best analogy to illustrate the incongruity of it all would be a family celebration at which everyone is enjoying a common joyful experience and then, as they assemble for the meal, the grandfather has to go change into a three-piece suit and use a podium to lead the praying of grace.

The story illustrates yet another effect of clericalization not mentioned in our prior descriptions. As the clergyhood of the ordained descends into clericalization, there is increased use of formal rituals that not only do not spring from the shared experience of the participants but even run counter to it. The more high ceremonial there is, the greater the risk of the ordained being experienced not as servants but as on a different plane, cut off from the body of priests they are called to serve. Rituals are symbolic in nature and as such are always multilayered. They are acts of communication, and their actual impact depends on their reception by those who experience them. The effect intended by those who design and perform them may be drowned out by the impact of the context. It can reveal things the clergy may be almost incapable of seeing about themselves.

The vision of a shared priesthood has been further promoted through efforts at inviting the ordained to share their personal spiritual journeys with some of their confreres in intimate prayer groups. The best known example would be a movement like Jesu Caritas groups.

Once again, it is surely true that many individual ordained priests have a priests' support group to thank for their ability to remain committed to their calling. Some ordained priests have regained a lost sense of that same commitment through such sharing, in the face of great interior struggle. It is a wonderful example of the desired integration of clergyhood with baptismal priesthood. That said, it need not imply a criticism if one were to ask a different question. Would it not contribute more to the solidarity of the faith community if the same kind of faith sharing that occurs in a priests' group were to be modeled by the ordained when they gather with the laity as peers on the journey of faith? We will explore that kind of vulnerability in chapters 5 and 6, when we look at possible remedies for healing clericalism in the ordained.

The Rituals at Presbyteral Ordination

Another example which illustrates the potential for clericalization is the pageantry which has grown up around the basic rite of priestly ordination in recent decades. Those who have not attended an ordination recently may be unaware of the accretions that have become expected practice across the country. The resulting spectacle is a timpanist's dream. From the trumpet fanfare that announces the beginning of the entry procession one would not be surprised if the ordinands were to enter on prancing steeds and bearing jousting lances.

This is not intended as some sort of jeremiad against liturgical exaltation. It is not a call for joyless sobriety in worship. Drama is an integral element in good liturgy, as the grand master Josef Jungmann always emphasized. Even pageantry can indeed be an appropriate part of an extraordinary and highly celebratory ecclesiastical event. The opening of an ecumenical council or a diocesan synod, which are joyful expressions of the entire church gathered in prayer for the special gifts of the Holy Spirit, might easily come to mind. The Eucharist is of course always an act of the whole church, but such events are more evidently actions of the whole community in solidarity. Still, pageantry is one thing, clerical triumphalism quite another. Do these recently developed ordination rituals give appropriate expression to what is supposedly taking place when someone is being called forth by the church to a life of ministerial service of the priestly people? The official ritual calls for the ordinand to prostrate himself in humility on the church floor, which is a challenging sign indeed. The ordinand is being called to servanthood, to death to self. But what effect might be reasonably anticipated when the rest of the elements of the ceremony are all but shouting at him that he must be pretty hot stuff if people went out of their way to put on a show like this for him? The contrast with the example of Jesus in stripping down and washing the feet of his disciples is jarring: "You call me 'teacher' and 'master,' and rightly so, for indeed I am. If I, therefore, the master and teacher, have washed your feet, you ought to wash one another's feet" (John 13:13).

The reality of the clericalization involved is heightened by the fact that these over-the-top practices are apparently not even subjected to conscious evaluation. They are taken for granted, which is exactly what is meant by an unexamined attitude, the telltale sign of clericalism. The practices are characteristic of a culture that has become second nature, even though it is out of sync with the essential meaning intended by the rite. On one occasion I suggested that the whole phenomenon of triumphalist ordinations might be at the very least incongruous. The planners' response was unconsciously quite instructive. They said, "the laypeople love it." That is also a perfect illustration of the complicity of the laity in the formation of a clericalized culture. (The planners, by the way, don't actually test whether the laypeople love it. I have frequently sat among the laity at such celebrations and observed their reactions. Their initial excitement at the fact that one of their relatives or friends is being ordained often turns to fidgeting and rolled eyes as the pomp goes on and on.)

An Irony

The church's recent emphasis on the corporate character of Holy Orders reveals a certain irony. Until Vatican II one heard little or nothing about the shared ministry of the ordained. Why did the fathers of the council feel the need to give heightened emphasis to this facet of ordained ministry? One reasonable conjecture: they urged this line of thinking precisely because priests up to then didn't act as if they were joined, in any genuinely interdependent sense, in a single collaborative mission. What was much more common then was the model of each pastor reigning in isolation within his own territorial fiefdom. (The minority bishops at Vatican I, those who resisted proclaiming the doctrine of papal infallibility, were on the wrong side theologically. But they proved to be better prophets than the infallibilists. They predicted, accurately as it turned out, the pastoral consequences of such a proclamation. In effect, they said that if the church proclaimed that the pope, even in very strictly limited conditions, could *teach* infallibly, it would not be long before the faithful would be saying he *was* infallible. And not long after that the virus of creeping infallibilism would lead to every village pastor being seen—and seeing himself—as infallible.)

One might logically expect those who enter into a clerical group to see themselves as joined together by their common calling. One would think the members would become collegial and interdependent. Such an attitude would represent the best side of clergification. But to live out of that attitude requires give-and-take; it requires trust and mutuality. It involves costly death to one's self-interest in order to priest. Sadly, all too often the deforming process of clericalization was allowed to permeate the ordained. Instead of the solidarity in action that might have been hoped for, the individual presbyter became the self-sufficient pastor.

Unexamined Attitude

Clergy: "I have been ordained. That gives me all I need for my flock. I don't need anything from the other guys tending their flocks."

Laity: "Why should we at suburban St. Mark's be concerned with the problems of inner-city or rural parishes?"

The isolation of the pastor shaped the isolation of the parish. People recited every Sunday a creed which declared their membership in a church that was one, holy, catholic, and apostolic. They proudly supported Peter's Pence. They knew they were linked to the figure that held it all together, the pope. But beyond profession of the same faith and participation in the same absolutely uniform rituals, there were precious few signs that a faith community in the inner city or out in the boonies, or the one down the street, might have a claim on them. Each parish was an island linked by its own causeway to Rome. The other islands could fend for themselves.

One of the graces coming out of the growing shortage of ordained priests has been the painful recognition that no parish is an island. Communities and their pastors are learning that they need one another, that collaboration is not an extra. It is of the essence of the community of the church. The pastor of the future-already-present has to make difficult adjustments in his attitudes and self-identification as he attempts to serve the leadership needs of two, three, four—or more—faith communities. And the folks in the pews will face a corresponding conversion from their insular understanding of what church is about.

A Return to Our Original Question

Our study originated in the attempt to understand the sexual misconduct scandal. We began with the observation that simply repeating the mantra, "it was the result of the clerical culture," is not very helpful. In the chapters that followed we recast the issues in two significant ways: by situating the clergyhood of the ordained within the broader context of clergyhood in general, and by situating the priesthood of the baptized as the reality which grounds the call to ordained ministry. In the light of that broader context and suggested reframing of the issue, we return to the sexual misconduct events that occasioned our questioning in the first place. How did the various clergies play their roles in the drama?

II

Tragedy and Transformation

Chapter Four
The Sexual Abuse Tragedy and the Clergies that Enacted It

We have explored the nature of clerical cultures. We noted their positive contributions to human meaning and order, as well as the potential they possess for generating attitudes and behaviors that are destructive of human community. In the case of the ordained practice of ministry to the Lord's people, we situated clergyhood within the fundamental call of every church member—without exception or distinction—to strive for the fullness of holiness demanded of a priestly people. With these concepts in place, we are in a better position to ask just what has taken place in the recent painful saga of sexual misconduct in the church.

A reader might be inclined to ask at this point, "Why do this? Why do we have to keep talking about this sorry blot on our church's life?" Or perhaps, "What does it have to do with me? I'm not part of the scandal."

We need to do it for at least three reasons. First, although you or I may not have been one of the onstage players in the story, something deeply affecting us as a church did happen to each of us. What happened is very painful and that pain may tempt us to want to bury it, which is never a healthy response. The effort to understand the meaning of painful experiences may cause us to confront things about our church (and ourselves) that we'd rather not face, when actually it is facing reality that offers the best hope of being healed of those patterns that contributed to our complicity in the events. The truth makes us free.

We need to reenter the story for another reason as well: to increase our understanding. The drama was/is a complex one, with multiple issues interwoven in the single story. In such a situation, with passions and possible prejudgments tugging at us from all sides, it is important to try to maintain perspective by reentering the story from various places, lest our feelings about particular moments in the saga skew the meaning of it all. We can easily exaggerate the importance of one component while overlooking the importance of others that might be equally significant. Half-truths don't make us free; they only create the illusion of freedom while reinforcing our biases.

And finally, we need to review the story because it helps our understanding of multiple clergies intersecting simultaneously, and therefore our appreciation of the dynamics of clericalism. Many people exercised power at different moments in the single story. The abuse of power took more than one form.

To be sure, we are all too close to the events to create the dispassionate narrative that historians will attempt to derive some decades from now. Feelings on all sides, whether those of the abused, the abusers, the various authority figures, or the church public in general, are too raw for that.

On the other hand, even at this early stage a variety of participants are putting forth different versions that purport to be "the story." Indeed, as is commonly the case with human tragedies, this immediate aftermath period might best be understood as a struggle for the power to name the whole experience.

What follows is, accordingly, a very tentative enterprise. It is offered as one person's modest attempt, working from the perspective of organizational systems, to address some facets of the story that have not been heard in the public conversation thus far. My hope is that shining a flashlight on these ideas might help us loosen ever so slightly positions we may have already adopted while wrestling with the pain of the immediate experience. Premature closure of interpretation not only blocks the possibility of growth, but it can also help to perpetuate the patterns that gave rise to the tragedy in the first place.

The Players

When dramas are enacted on the physical stage, we meet individual players enacting unique parts. Any one of them might also happen to have a public role in their particular society: a king, perhaps, or president, a fading movie star or a salesman. The sexual misconduct story is, on one level, quite similar. Individual priests abused the individual children of particular parents and families; individual bishops made particular choices to deal with each individual accusation against each individual priest. Father John Geoghan's story is different from Father Paul Shanley's, and Father Rudy Kos has yet another. Cardinal Bernard Law was not Cardinal Roger Mahony. And the United States bishops are not the Vatican. In that sense each individual story is unique.

But each is also a manifestation of broader realities at work. This book began with the assessment that, at least in the case of the ordained, a whole cultural matrix with its unexamined but operative assumptions made a collective contribution to the unfolding of the story. Now, in the light of our further reflections, we need to take into account that there were other *groups* playing significant *collective* roles in the drama. They may not quite qualify as clergy. They do not all exhibit every characteristic attached to that title. But we won't understand the story if we neglect the corporate impact they had on the drama. Beyond the level of individual agency, the story is one of *multiple human systems rubbing against one another,* each with its own cultural patterns. Each came to the single unfolding story with its own assumptions and expectations and interests, acknowledged or not.

The drama unfolded in stages, with different mini-cultures appearing in the person of particular players. Perhaps the best way to appreciate the dynamics of the entire drama is to see it unfolding as a series of discrete acts.

Act One: The Abusive Actions

It is worth reminding ourselves that at the first moment (though that moment was repeated, sadly, in numbers of instances that are mind-numbing) there were only two players involved: an abusing priest and an innocent young boy or girl. Their actions take place offstage. In fact, it would be accurate to say that at this moment the stage is dark. At this point there are no bishops on the stage; there are no parents; there are no victim advocates; there are no lawyers or insurance personnel; there are no media; there is no USCCB and no Vatican; and there is no general public, either ecclesial or societal.

Why is it important to keep this in mind? Because it helps us to appreciate that in a real sense the drama had several successive beginnings. In many instances these starting points occurred long after the individual acts of sexual abuse. Had each of those original actions remained a secret between the priest perpetrator and his victim, the event would still have had the traumatizing and tragic impact it had in the life of each child. The initial acts of the abusive priests and the bishops who covered up their behavior remain the catalyst and center for everything else that followed, to be sure. We must never lose sight of that central reality. But without further choices by other members of other guilds none of the other participants in the story would have made it to the stage. The story would have ended there. From that perspective the full story, though it has its origins and center in the abusive—decidedly unpriestly—actions themselves, is largely a function of *the reactions of the rest of the cast once they learn of their occurrence.* Individual persons—and collective groups—made choices that were not necessitated by the original evil acts. They chose what meaning to give to what they learned, and they chose the course of action they would initiate on the basis of that meaning. In every instance they could have chosen otherwise and the resulting story would have turned out quite differently. The full story is not titled: *"Acts of Sex Abuse Against Children."* Nor is it even *"Sex Abuse of Children by Priests; Cover-up by Bishops."* It might be titled: *"Sex Abuse of Children by Priests, Cover-up by Bishops, the Actions Taken by Other Societal Players, Lawsuits, the Charter, Public Exposure—and How We Choose to Respond to the Story as It has been Reported to Us."*

We turn first, then, to the incidents of abuse themselves. To "Act One." It is generally accepted that the men who perpetrated the actual acts of abuse were psychologically stunted in some way or other. I leave it to mental health professionals to pinpoint the exact nature of the compulsions or addictions at work in them, but laypeople use the generic word "sick." The psychological community lends support to such a view when it takes the position that in the case of these men recidivism is highly probable if not certain, at least in the case of true pedophiles, i.e., those who abuse prepubescent children. Their freedom *not* to act out is somehow impaired or deficient. In some instances the disorder can compel them to become predators, consciously and repeatedly seeking out victims and not simply responding to occasional and momentarily uncontrollable impulses.

This is perhaps the best place to recall that none of us is in a position to judge the moral guilt of any of these priests. That is a matter for the priest's own conscience, the sacred ground where he faces his God, exactly as each of us must. When we in society make the evaluation that the man's freedom was or was not impaired, we are only using the best prudential tools available to us for determining society's judgment of responsibility or criminality.

The fact that the disorder was personal to each of the perpetrators does not of itself, however, eliminate the potential causative impact of the clerical culture upon his actions. Our actions as humans are a function of the interplay between, on the one hand, the societal conditioning that has shaped us and, on the other, our responses to that conditioning. The fact that not every priest responded to the potentially destructive tendencies inherent in the clerical culture—haughty disdain for outsiders, imperviousness to critique, an exaggerated sense of entitlements, etc.—does not mean those tendencies can be treated as negligible in appreciating why these particular men acted out in the way they did. The dark potential of the ordained clerical culture contributed to the abuse of power by the offending priests (and subsequently, the offending bishops) as surely as each man's own inner conflicts did.

Next we turn to the other characters in Act One, the children. They too are unfree, not because of any psychological defect but for two different reasons. Society judges that their emotional development is too immature to allow them freely to consent to what these spiritual authority figures are doing to them. More importantly, in addition to age, the lack of freedom in these young boys and girls is compounded by the abuse of power on the part of an adult in a superior position. That power imbalance makes the actions both possible and particularly abhorrent.

What follows may come as a hard saying for the victims, but a full understanding of the story demands that it be included. The same clerical culture that shaped the consciousness of the perpetrating priests was also operative in the vulnerability of the young people to these acts, and made it especially difficult to break the shell of silence after they had occurred. This is a delicate area, for sure. In no way am I imputing *guilt* on the victims' part for what was done to them. What I am saying is that the way they viewed the priest was a function of a particular version of the clerical culture. It necessarily contributed to the way they accepted the messages the priest gave as he seduced them. In no way can they be said to be responsible for that conditioning. The image of the all-holy priest set them up. It came through the medium of parents and others who "taught" them how to view priests—a conditioning those adults had accepted from their own upbringing in a particular church milieu.

The children were clearly victims of individual men, but they were also victims of an ideology. That ideology, the unchallenged view of the ordained priest as some dis-incarnate sacred figure untouched by human frailty, conditioned them to place their trust in the man even as they experienced his behavior to be contradicting that lofty image and expectation. In some instances the power of the ideology held the child in its thrall after repeated acts of abuse over a period of years. How could this man be doing anything wrong? He was the living representative of Christ himself. The confluence of their immature age, a utopian sacred image, and a conflicting sense that something very wrong was happening, constituted the perfect emotional storm for these young people. They were being compelled to participate in acts they had been taught to hold mortally sinful, and then, after the acts had occurred, how free could the children possibly be to challenge the powerful ideology ingrained in their parents?

We need to round out our presentation of the story by noting that the clerical culture would not have had the same impact on the psyche of every individual victim. Just as not every ordained minister is shaped by the culture in exactly the same fashion, so too with the laity. Not every young person was imprinted to the same degree with that set of predisposing orientations, whether of the person of the ordained or of the meaning of sexual behavior itself. The meaning each individual child attached to the notion of "priest" would have come, to some extent, from formal church catechesis; but it would have been more powerfully imprinted by the way the child's parents and family actually interacted with the real priests in their experience. We develop our most profound attitudes by imitating the most significant figures in our lives.

We leave the events in Act One with the sense that the clerical culture played at least *some* role in the actions of the abusing priests and the belief systems that made their young victims particularly vulnerable. In the absence of such an idealized image, the response of the young person in the situation might have been quite different. The likelihood of active resistance would have been much greater. The figure of "the holy pastor"—Catholics call their priests "Father," after all—holds enormous power, and this imbalance of power is at the heart of things when people speak of the "clerical culture" in this situation.

Act Two: The Secret Doesn't Hold

The second act in the story also takes place "offstage." Conversations take place and we who were not privy to them can only rely on our judgment of the trustworthiness of those who eventually tell us what took place. The clerical culture again shapes, at least in part, what happens in this act. The players have choices to make. Some act out of their calling and lives as priests, while the actions of others are poisoned by attitudes of clericalism. Sadly, the public spotlight focuses only on the clericalized. Priestly behavior is left in the shadows. It's not a scandal.

One fact we can be sure of is that at some point the secrecy about the acts that took place in Act One was over. Victims broke the taboo that had held them bound. They told someone. It might have been a parent, or a teacher, or a friend. It could have been another priest. And the telling could have taken place on the next day or twenty years after the fact. The important point is that the message now reaches the ear of a bishop or major superior. At that point the story is not yet up on the public stage, but we are getting close.

If the early confidant of the victim was a priest, we are introduced to a second representative of the clergy. And here a significant thing happens. We now know that some of the ordained did indeed act as priests. They resisted the clericalized tendency to deny or avoid the reality. Despite their deep qualms of conscience at possibly being disloyal to their superiors, they refused to be complicit in the abuse. They spoke out and named what their brother priest was doing. They took the matter to their bishop. They may not have gone to civil authorities at that point.[1] Perhaps as a result of the clergy cocoon, they were unaware of that civic responsibility. One of the operating assumptions engendered by the clericalization of the ordained is: "Because we are religious, we are not accountable to society the way other citizens are." But at least some spoke up. They may remain unseen by the public, but we can hope that they have the satisfaction of knowing they did the courageous, priestly thing.

In other cases the matter arrived on the bishop's desk directly from the layperson who received the initial confidence, such as a

---

1. Neither did the parents or others to whom the children risked telling their story. Is this another example of misplaced loyalty ("you just don't wash the church's dirty linen in public")? Or perhaps a more hopeful interpretation is that they wanted to start healing through relationship, not immediately enter the world of crime and punishment.

parent or teacher. In still others it was brought to the bishop's (or major superior's) attention by the actual individual who had been abused.

In any case, the ordained clergy have now joined the cast of Act Two. They are present in the persons of those most responsible for the identity and patterns of its local chapter, the bishops. The question at this point in the drama, when the events are still not in the public consciousness, is: will the bishop priest? Will he act as his own person with the integrity of the Gospel call to relationship? Or will he allow the assumptions of a clerical culture to determine his response? Will he intervene as a person in relationship, or will he cloak himself in the impersonality of a role?

In light of the failures that became evident once the stage lights were turned on for Act Three, it is important to keep in mind that some bishops did indeed simply allow themselves to be directly vulnerable to the pain of the abused. They spoke with the victims' parents or, in the case of later disclosure, with the abused themselves. They asked forgiveness and they offered any help the abused sought in order to redress the wrong. In at least one diocese I am aware of, the bishop, years before the explosive revelations in Boston, had created a board with the responsibility to investigate as soon as a charge of abuse was reported. The board was made up predominantly of laymen and women, including therapists, social workers, and at least two victims. The bishop treated every recommendation of the board as his marching orders. Bishops of that sort never appear on the public stage at all. Because they acted as priests, the victims experienced some measure of healing, and the drama ended with reconciliation. (It should also be noted that in the early '90s the body of bishops as a whole had taken serious steps toward putting national policies in place to forestall repetition of the experiences unearthed earlier. Apparently the assumption was that policy formulations would do the job all by themselves, which is another very clerical misunderstanding. Policies don't administer themselves.)

Before the curtain opens on Act Three, it is important to examine what went on in the case of those bishops who chose a different course. Important, because the central reality of Act Two is the cover-up and mishandling of allegations, which resulted in further acts of abuse. Who did those bishops talk to? And what did they do with the responses they received?

As a rule, laypeople are completely in the dark about the structures that might come into play when a personnel issue lands on a bishop's desk. The first thing to note is that there is no absolutely uniform procedure. Most dioceses will have, at least on paper, a priests' personnel board a bishop might consult. Some of the larger dioceses have a priest in an executive role as director of priest personnel. In reality, every bishop is free to decide what significance he will attach to any advice he might seek from any such structure. Some bishops would typically share the matter privately with a man on their immediate administrative team, such as a vicar general or chancellor. Yet another bishop might keep it totally to himself and make the eventual decision about what action to take without consulting anyone. The one bottom line common to all such structures is that they are purely advisory. The bishop is not bound by any advice he might choose to seek. Legally, that is. The requirements of wisdom or even simple prudence are another matter.

Be that as it may, when the curtain finally opens on Act Three we will learn a new and distressing fact. Some bishops (not all, we must continually remind ourselves in the face of the generalizations that bombarded us in the media) did move priests known to be guilty of abuse from one assignment to another. It is possible (though unknowable in the absence of a public hearing) that some were so far out of touch that they took no preventive measures at all and simply gave the man a token exhortation and finger-wagging. Frequently, perhaps in the majority of instances, they acted after taking what they judged to be sufficient steps to minimize the likelihood of further acts of abuse, as inadequate as those steps proved to be.

In any case the power of their conditioning to clericalization becomes evident. The steps they took were naive and misguided.

The Effects of a Pietistic Spirituality

In an interview given early on in the public crisis Bishop Joseph Galante, acting as a spokesman for the U.S. bishops, said that in the 1970s or '80s bishops thought acts of sexual abuse against minors were sins, and didn't treat them as crimes.

Fair enough. The ignorance of the criminal nature of the offense and the lack of concern for the young person involved may be judged inexcusable, but they acted out of their cultural conditioning. In their eyes what happened was sin, moral failure. Even if we accept their limited grasp of the situation, we need to examine their mode of response, because it reveals important aspects of their spirituality.

How did they deal with the sin? What was their most frequent response? Get the offender off to a monastery. Have him make a retreat and go to confession. Get him back to prayer. And if we do have to pay some respect to the helping professions, at least let it be in a Catholic facility.

This is a spirituality that is both at odds with the doctrine of the Incarnation, so central to Christianity, and based on faulty assumptions. First, its approach to prayer is totally instrumental, making God a utility for redressing our failings. A prescription of prayer becomes a tool for avoidance and blame, not entrance into deeper conversion and communion. Furthermore, this approach fails to recognize the psychological obsessions, compulsions, projections, and all the other mechanisms that have an impact on the behavior of even the freest of us humans. The glory of our God is that the Lord works *through* human nature and the effects of sin, not through flight from them.

Such a spirituality is incapable of differentiating between destructive sympathy and hard-nosed empathy. The bishops' prevailing image was that powerful Christian icon, the Good Shepherd. There is a sad irony here. They thought they were being good shepherds to sinful men, but their disembodied spirituality left them completely unaware of how that revered image can easily be twisted. As those skilled in the treatment of addiction know from long experience, the well-intentioned but psychologically naive shepherd easily becomes the enabler of addictive and terribly destructive behavior.

If we need to see how effective this kind of pietistic spirituality is at merely masking deeper problems without solving them, we need look no further than the story of FBI agent Robert Hanssen. Driven by fear of the demons that tormented him (many having their origins in psychological abuse by his father), he sought salvation by committing himself totally to a pious organization, Opus Dei. It provided clear spiritual boundaries and protections. He attended Mass and received the Eucharist daily, participated in other religious practices regularly for years. And for those same years he collected pornographic literature, frequented prostitutes, and served as a Russian spy, causing the deaths of agency colleagues who trusted him even as he viewed them with utter disdain because he felt he was so superior in his craft.

Prayer does not always deal with reality. Spiritual practices can be a shield to avoid confronting deep and powerful psychological drives. Religiosity can be an escape from incredibly complex inner conflicts—which themselves may be so subtle as to escape detection by either the most accomplished therapist or the most astute spiritual director. For all our increased sophistication in matters both spiritual and psychological, the originating sources of human actions, good and bad, remain shrouded in profound mystery. God and the human are both grander than the pietistic spirituality the bishops brought to their ministry. The bishops' failure to recognize abuse by priests as a crime may or may not make them guilty in the eyes of the law; the feeble response they made to what they saw as sin would earn them a failing grade in any respectable program for training of spiritual directors. Pope John Paul II said that the present crisis "must lead to a holier priesthood, a holier episcopate and a holier church." Well and good, if the underlying notion of holiness is sound. All holiness involves humility. In this case it is the humility to recognize that the children of this world—psychiatric professionals—may be wiser than those who see themselves as the children of light.

The argument about the spirituality that was at play in the behavior of the bishops calls for an additional nuance, one directly touching on the issue of clericalism. That spirituality was itself one of the ideological components of the clerical culture that shaped the self-understanding of the offending priests. The assumption operative originally in Act One, that priests are disembodied representatives of Jesus, receives a codicil in the behavior of the pietistic bishops: "Priests are all-holy; they are not subject to the spiritual and emotional infirmities that beset the rest of humanity."

Act Two ends. The secrecy has been shattered and some bishops have yielded to the tendency inherent in every form of clericalization, by failing to treat the victims as persons and enabling perpetrators from within the guild to avoid the truth of their responsibility.

Act Three: Mobilization and Public Disclosure

The stage lights finally go up and the curtain is opened. The drama becomes public, revealed to the world in the media. We the public are made aware of the shocking story for the first time. We also discover that besides the victims, the abusing priests, and religious authorities, other players are now on the stage. Front and center, to be exact.

It turns out that after the bishops' responses, the victims refused to simply fade into the shadows. Instead they talked *to each other.* And they experienced the power of solidarity. They became more than a collection of aggrieved individuals. They decided to take action collectively, and in order to do that they brought two other sets of players into the story. They chose spokespersons and gave them the role of victims' advocates. And they enlisted the aid of another guild, the legal clergy.

To pay particular attention to these strategies does not mean to attack them. When past injustices have been reported and there has been no redress, it is a perfectly honorable next step to coalesce scattered individual forces and form a united front. No one should be faulted for choosing it. It may be the only way to redress injustice for those who feel themselves otherwise powerless, a priestly effort at achieving accountability and justice by breaking through the nonaccountability of clericalism. How that new power is then *exercised*, whether through tactics designed to promote healing or through measures which are themselves new forms of injustice and manipulation, can only be assessed in the aftermath. It is not our present concern, which is simply to validate the coalescence of power.

In any case, organization is not a neutral act. It creates a sense of agency in those who had been trapped in the illusion of impotence and perpetual victimhood. It introduces a new form of power into the drama: the power of solidarity. The choice to join forces and break the story publicly changes the dynamic essentially and will inevitably evoke reaction from the keepers of the status quo. (The sociologist Sister Maria Augusta Neale used to observe that surveys always show that the public strongly favors helping "the poor." But the support drops dramatically when the term is tweaked slightly and people are asked their reaction to "the *organized* poor." The public—those with power to change the situation—is quite willing to be benevolent toward individuals who are hurting; it gets nervous when they break through their isolation and bond to become a single agent.)

A personal experience illustrates the point: Some time after the public revelations had occurred, I was facilitating a conversation about its impact with the members of a diocesan pastoral council. After they had processed their assessments of the situation in small groups, one woman reported the sense of her group that "the victims' lobby has taken over."

A "lobby." "Taken over." The language indicates that the initiation of a concerted response has given rise to a new and negative interpretation of what is going on. Is the language too prejudicial? Or is it an accurate descriptor we might be afraid of using lest we be accused of victimizing the victims? Much depends on the tactics that will be used. However that may be, the one point to hold onto is that if the victims had *not* organized, nothing would have changed. The diseased culture would have prevailed.

In any case, the opening of the curtain with the disclosure of charges against the bishops has another effect. It implicates a further set of characters. It brings us, the community of the faithful, into the story. Knowledge of what has been allowed to go on makes us responsible in a new way. We will not be able to walk out of this theater unchanged by what we witness. Whether the destructive patterns continue or not now depends on how we respond to things we might have preferred to avoid knowing.

The Legal Clergy

A new clergy, in the persons of lawyers for the abused, is now visible up on the stage. That makes it possible for us to consider another component of that fraternity, one we have not seen up to now but which has already been at work behind the scenes during Act Two. They are the lawyers on the other side, the ones charged with advising church authorities. These lawyers represent the interest of the diocese or religious congregation.

We have already noted that it is a mistake to equate the clerical culture with the actions only of the ordained. When we consider those to whom the bishops turned as the mobilized victims were moving toward public action, that point comes home with full force. Once we move past the ordained clerics who might have advised the transfer of their fellow priests who were abusers, we meet those lawyers who advised the bishops on how to respond to the victims. They were generally not ordained. They were ordinarily laymen. And most probably good Catholics in the bargain. As such, they had their feet in two clerical cultures at once. They shared in the clericalized culture of the church as well as that of the legal profession. What kind of advice did they give? And what kind of a vision informed that advice?

Realize that by this point the focus of the drama has shifted. The victims have gone to their pastors first and been left unsatisfied. The decision to bring the conflict into the U.S. judicial system was made in good faith by victims who were frustrated by their inability to engage their local bishop in meaningful personal dialogue. But for all its good intention, that shift created an additional obstacle to the priestly healing we might have hoped for. The legal clergy come onto the stage with their own set of assumptions. Their training focuses their attention on promoting the financial interests and diminishing the liability of their clients. In the U.S. legal system people in a stressful conflict situation are pushed into becoming adversaries. The possibility of interpersonal (priestly) *relationship* among baptized brothers and sisters is all but destroyed, and money and even the possibility of criminal prosecution of bishops become front and center. All parties are propelled willy-nilly into the game that must be played by the rules of the legal culture.

Interestingly, the early church was quite skittish about Christians having recourse to the civil judicial system to resolve matters contested within the Christian community. Paul writes to the church at Corinth: "How can any one of you with a case against another dare to bring it to the unjust for judgment instead of to the holy ones? . . . Can it be that there is not one among you wise enough to be able to settle a case between brothers? But rather brother goes to court against brother, and that before unbelievers?" (1 Cor 6:1, 5-6). No doubt the concrete historical circumstances of a Roman imperial court are quite different from those in contemporary America, and Paul's view of the world outside the church as "wicked" must be viewed in light of that context. Still, the underlying mentality remains an intriguing challenge for a spirituality based on our baptismal relationship to one another. The same mentality is evidenced in the admonition of Jesus about the stages to be followed in the process of fraternal correction: you begin by direct personal effort at resolution of the difficulty; if that doesn't work you bring in another of the faithful; if that fails, bring it to the church—and only then "treat him as you would a Gentile or a tax collector" (Matt 18:15-17). (And even that final stage, which looks like unbridgeable separation, must be interpreted against the way Jesus himself dealt with Gentiles and tax collectors—with a predilection for their company!) Unfortunately, our knowledge of the actual conditions does not give us insight into the ways they might have held the leader of the community—a bishop, in today's church—accountable in a priestly fashion.

Be that as it may, the recourse to the law brings *two* sets of legal players to the stage. The drama is now less about the abusers and the victims, and more a struggle between two different roles played *within the legal guild itself.* One set of players is focused on securing the legitimate demands of the aggrieved. The other is concerned to protect the assets of the church against any unfair encroachment on what they judge to be its appropriate and legal interests. The two sets of lawyers may happen to be on different sides (for the present moment), but they are essentially playing the same game, enacting a single drama: protecting competing interests by arguing for conflicting interpretations of legal precedents. It is really accidental that each set of lawyers happens to be on one side rather than the other. Today's lawyers for the victims might be tomorrow's lawyers for the diocese. Both are imprinted with the positive strengths, but also the potentially destructive tendencies of their clerical culture. That culture (at least in its American version) gets the very air it needs to survive from the continuation of conflict.

Unexamined Attitude

Legal Clergy: "Only my client's interests count."

And those interests are conceived almost exclusively in monetary terms. The restoration of human, much less baptismal, relationships between the parties has been cast into the background.

In the case of the diocesan attorneys, it can be reasonably asked how much they allowed the priesting imperatives of the Gospel to challenge the normal responsibility-evading tactics of most secular leaders. In that world counselors advise leaders never to acknowledge responsibility for their actions, because such an admission can be used against them. Cloak yourself with "I don't recall" or "that was a different time" and it may all go away. You have to protect the image of your organization above all. One of the sad ironies is that the frantic efforts to avoid scandal actually scandalized a knowing faithful as much or even more than the pathetic acts of abuse themselves.

If I may be permitted a slight diversion at this point, the very public story of the charge against Joseph Cardinal Bernardin offers insight from two different angles. It presents us with the example of a pastor who resisted the mind-set of his own legal counsel and retained his sense of his own personhood and priesthood, illustrating the glaring contrast with the behavior of those bishops who succumbed to clericalism. And it reminds us of the ever-present possibility of false accusation. You may recall the story.

When Bernardin was accused of sexual misconduct by Stephen Cook, the legal community offered him the same kind of counsel they gave to other bishops in the public spotlight amid accusations of sexual misconduct: If you must talk before the media at all—and it's better if you can avoid it completely—do so only with a prepared text, and answer no questions off-the-cuff. And by no means allow yourself to risk a face-to-face meeting with your accuser. What you say could be used against you in his suit.

Their admonitions are a classic example of the clerical mind-set that, in its efforts to protect against legal and monetary liability, advises the abandonment of every potential for the human, interpersonal dialogue that might promote healing. Bernardin was made of better stuff. He chose a different, baptismal route, as we know. He confronted the situation. He stood before the press, spoke as the words came to him, and gave direct answers to any question they chose to ask. He was naked, not hiding behind some cloak of imputed dignity. He invited Stephen to talk with him as brother to brother.

Bernardin's pastoral response led this troubled young man to retract his false accusation. The cardinal acted in a way which protected Stephen's dignity as it reversed the media machine's thirst for scandal. The world knows the respect and admiration he garnered by his behavior, not only for himself but for the restoration of trust and hope for the integrity of the church.

Returning to the collective story line, we must, in fairness to the diocesan attorneys, note that another factor had come into play at this point. The financial patrimony of the people in the pews was at stake. The bishops are stewards of that money, responsible for protecting it. And legal suits were on the table. The church leaders found themselves confronted with a Hobson's choice: admit their culpability and forfeit the resources needed to fund programs to carry out the church's mission, or put up a barrier of non-accountability and legal sleight of hand to save what can be saved. It is part of the human tragedy that failure to acknowledge a painful reality at an earlier stage—failure to priest—only results in a steeper price later on. If one removes the victims from the story (as if that were possible or desirable) it becomes easier to see that the leaders were faced with shame no matter which course they chose. We can only wonder what advice their lawyers (themselves much conditioned by the pressure of still other lawyers representing the insurance industry) gave the bishops. Perhaps any diocesan lawyer who would recommend honest confrontation of the facts might have found himself without a job.

The legal clergyhood is present also in the other set of lawyers, those representing the abused in their search for justice. Two reports heard offstage and departing from the proclaimed script may shed a darker light on that whole enterprise.

Is It Really about Justice?

The first was shared with me by a layman (not a lawyer) who had the responsibility of managing the abuse cases for a metropolitan diocese. When I asked him about the situation he replied: "We know that when the first story broke the lawyers in town went and got the yearbooks of every Catholic high school in the city for the past forty years and began systematically to call each graduate to ask him if he had ever been abused."

It's a single anecdote, to be sure, but it bears an uncanny resemblance to another account, shared with me by the financial officer of an international religious community. He was likewise involved in tracking the situation for the congregation: "We know that early on there were a couple of international gatherings of lawyers convened by some of the more visible American firms. At the first meeting the convener said in effect, 'Guys, the cash cow for the next seven years is the Catholic Church. Go get 'em.'"

I am quite aware of the risk that either of these men might simply be defending the organization he was working for. Still, in each instance my own knowledge of the man telling me the story leads me to trust the reality of what they were both alleging. It would not be the first instance of the kind of ambulance chasing that is an occupational hazard of the legal clergy.

Unfortunately, the effect of such tactics is not merely the lining of the lawyers' pockets, as grubby as that is. Seeking out potential clients in that manner opens the door for opportunists willing to conveniently recover some memories in return for potentially large remuneration. The whole issue of justice becomes tainted.

When lawyers troll through the rolls of society in search of possible victims (who become their actual clients), their greed increases the likelihood that two further forms of injustice will occur. First there is the probability that the reputations of some innocent people (in this instance, pastors) will be irreparably harmed by false testimony. And second, the credibility of those who were actually abused becomes subject to further attack by being lumped together with that same false testimony.

We are not in a position to charge any individual with false testimony against priests. As persons, that is a matter for individual consciences; in the civic realm it is the business of the courts. But anyone with a modicum of awareness of how such things work on the larger stage of human society knows how naive it is to imagine that every individual who came forth with a claim of having been abused had actually been violated. This reality does not, of course, minimize the huge number of proven cases and the serious cultural reality crying out for explanation. But the high probability that false claims have been made and innocent priests' reputations destroyed on the basis of them demands that it be included in the whole catalog. In recent times we have in fact begun to hear of priests now being restored to ministry after their cases were investigated and no grounds were found for condemning them. Whether the shadow of suspicion unjustly cast upon them can ever be erased and their lives made whole is an open question. Those who were violated physically, it turns out, were not the only victims. The clericalism of some in the legal fraternity worked its own harm by proactively stimulating the likelihood of phony claims. In doing so they indirectly impugned the credibility of those victims who came forward with genuine grievances: some of the supposed victims were clearly lying, so the genuine ones could be, too. Real victims are further victimized by the presentation of phony claims.

Another reality not noted in the official script is the hard calculation that out of all the huge sums paid out by the church, a sizable amount ended up in the pockets of the lawyers. Thirty percent is the generally accepted figure; the treasurer of the international congregation mentioned above placed it closer to sixty percent. The victims might be excused if they wonder what all the rhetoric of "justice for the abused" was really all about.

To sum up. The entrance of the legal clergy completed the process of closing the door to the possibility of priestly relationship and restitution. A search for human communion was transmuted into a demand for the poor substitute of financial compensation. And the clericalism of some of the legal clergy led to further victimization of innocent persons. And it was all done in the name of justice.

The Media Clergy

Although the lights are now up on the set, it may be difficult for the audience to sort out the ever larger cast. The glare of flashbulbs popping all around the stage makes it hard to know who's who. Reporters with notebooks are everywhere. Microphones are being thrust into other players' faces. Act Three brings us the media clergy too.

What role do the media play in the sex abuse drama? Of course they tell us *about* the events as they unfold. But beyond that, in a real sense they are not just neutral observers who happen to be up on the stage; they are players *in* the story as well. They may not be victims or abusers or church authorities or their advisors, but their reporting affects the way we are brought into the story. By what they say and show—as well as what they choose not to say or to conceal—they shape our perceptions and thus our experience. In effect, they tell us who is important and who is not; whose words deserve attention and whose can be glossed over; what details count and which are simply window dressing.

The media are a powerful clergyhood. They have their own club rules and expectations and taboos. The slogan on the masthead of the *New York Times* famously reads "All the news that's fit to print." It may represent their ideal. But when wags turn it into "All the news that fits we print," they are alerting us in a playful way that it is also an ideology covering its own unacknowledged biases. Cable TV, with its 24-hour news cycle, and the Internet and blogosphere, leave the public even more exposed to reckless and unverified information: sound bites.

The media clergy can be seen moving back and forth among the members of the other clergyhoods who are trying to spin the story one way or another. "The lawyer for the victims claimed. . ." "The spokesperson for the archdiocese refused to comment." "The SNAP representative, herself an abuse victim, charged . . ." Each word of each sentence grabs our lapels and tugs us in one direction or another. Each statement is an exercise of power, however objective it purports to be.

Unexamined Attitude

Media Clergy: "Blood sells. Keep the provocative content in front of them and they won't ask about how power is being used."

How has the media behaved in telling this story? I have heard voices of lay Catholics bewailing the unfair press: "When are they going to stop beating on the church?" One prince of the church suggested that the publishing of a grand-jury report was the act of anti-Catholics. I have also heard the voices of priests who acknowledge that the media has done the church a service simply by playing its appropriate role in society.

Why is it important for us who are the audience to pay attention to things like the uses of power by the media, when it seems we can't really do anything about them? Because the cultural transformation to be outlined in chapters 5 and 6 will require changed behavior from every one of us. If we are to write the new scripts, we need to be aware of the societal forces that continue to reinforce old ones. Two examples will suffice to illustrate the kind of judgment we in the audience need to exercise as we determine the kind of role we may be called to play in creating the story line of the future.

First, Boston. Long before the story of sexual misconduct by priests broke, I had heard people from Beantown say that *The Boston Globe* "has it in" for the Catholic Church. Those of us with little personal experience of life in Boston can only say, "Perhaps—or perhaps not." The Catholic Church bestrides Boston like the Colossus of Rhodes. It is quite possible that its dominance might give rise to snarky and unwarranted efforts to put the church in its place. On the other hand, it's just as possible that such comments are only the church's embarrassment at getting caught. Bostonians are the only ones licensed to discern their own motivations.

Then came Philadelphia. Two years after the first disclosures in Boston (and over two decades after the first case in Louisiana, when the canary in the mine had ominously stopped singing), the *Philadelphia Inquirer* stirred up the pot when it published the complete report of the district attorney on all the actions of sixty-three priests. Once again there were those, priests and laity alike, who took the position that these were public records and so be it. Others took the report as a cheap shot designed to support an aggressive, headline-grabbing district attorney in her effort to get the state's statute of limitations extended so more cases could be prosecuted and she could advance her political career. Still others felt the paper was playing its proper societal role, but remarked,

"Did they *really* have to publish all those graphic details in a paper that might be read by kids?"

It will take a lot of analysis by those skilled in media watching to come to a balanced assessment of the way the media played its role in the story. Within the guild itself some may earn roses and others onions. The important thing for us, the audience of baptized priests, is to have the spiritual sophistication to be aware of the kinds of interests at play as the story is spun. Scandal sells papers. And continued scandal sells lots more.

To conclude these reflections on the legal clergy and the media clergy, then. Neither were *the* problem. Nor should they be faulted for entering the story. Lawyers were called to the stage by bishops and victims; by their vocation the media bear the responsibility of helping society understand significant events in its unfolding story. The point is that their entry did introduce further manifestations of power. Their respective clergyhoods each brought with them both the potential for positive service to the public and their own particular tendencies toward (perhaps unconscious) abuse of power. The more dispassionate judgment of history will judge how well they contributed to truth and justice and resisted the tendencies of clericalism.

The offending bishops had not acted in a priestly manner. Recourse to the legal community had removed the process from the potential for the interpersonal to the sure consequences of the adversarial. And the media lost the story of the collective religious tragedy as it focused the public's attention on the bathos of one more trial of the century.

But perhaps more importantly, our review of their roles will help us not simply to react or join polarized "sides," but think more clearly about what the tragedy means to us as a community of faith, a royal priesthood. The bottom line is that we need to get beyond the clericalizing hazards of all the clergies involved if we are going to assume our responsibility for the future of the community of faith.

Act Three has drawn toward its close. The story had been greatly determined by its presentation up on the major stages. Boston, Los Angeles, Portland, and Philadelphia stand out. But it was also unfolding in other dioceses across the country. To do justice to the story we would have to imagine a set designer's dream: hundreds of scenes taking place on separate diocesan stages simultaneously.

The story, once again, could have played itself out quite differently than what eventually happened. It might have worked its way to separate endings in each of those dioceses. Each individual bishop would then have been judged in the local court of public opinion. (And truth to tell, the assessment would have been made as much on the basis of the particular bishop's prevailing mode of relationship to his people as on his performance in the abuse situation itself. Bernard Law's disconnect with the faithful of Boston didn't begin with his handling of the abuse cases. A contrasting story of another member of the hierarchy makes the point. When Rembert Weakland fell, many of the faithful of Milwaukee accepted it as a tragic flaw in a much admired churchman, as demonstrated when he admitted his sin and publicly asked forgiveness of the faithful. The record of his previous relationship to the people in the pews generated a much different outcome. It's really no different than what happens in the secular world, incidentally. When Martha Stewart is exposed, she already brings with her a reputation as either a diva or a harridan. When Sammy Sosa corks his bat he's not a cheater, but our lovable teddy bear.)

In any event, once again a choice is made. The sheer multitude of local stories cannot remain isolated from one another; even without the extensive media coverage, the contagion would have spread and become a national narrative. The media simply speeded up the process. The hierarchy came to the conclusion that it had no other choice than to shape a unified national response. The curtain brings Act Three to a close; the stage hands do their magic; the curtain goes up once more. And we all find ourselves in Dallas.

Act Four: The Charter

In theory it was conceivable that each diocesan story would have remained just that, and there would have been no Act Four.

After all, each bishop made his own choices and created his own story independently. But of course in the real world that ending had become impossible. The age of self-contained villages with impermeable boundaries ended with the invention of tom-toms and smoke signals. Airwaves know no fences. The many stories had become a single story and the separate diocesan audiences had become one. The audience was the nation, and indeed the world.

The bishops clearly had to act as a body. The policies enacted in the early '90s may have been well crafted, but like all policies they simply marked out boundaries. In policy matters everything depends on the human beings charged with implementing them. (We can only imagine the appropriate anger that must have been felt by those bishops who had confronted the reality with integrity—as priests—from the first moment. They had done no wrong, but they were compelled to share in the work of creating a collective response. They had to participate at Dallas, willy-nilly. Corporate solidarity can exact a heavy price in return for its benefits.)

The high drama of the bishops' extraordinary meeting illustrates one more manifestation of the power of the clerical culture. For the laity it was still a matter of "What are *the bishops* going to do about this?" The notion that a more appropriate question might be "What are *we* going to do?" was not on the radar of most laypeople. The mentality of shared responsibility for their church had not been part of the catechesis that they had been taught to accept without question.

Be that as it may, the bishops perpetuated the clericalism of the system in two ways. First, by the very method they used in reaching their decisions, they left out any public consultation of the laity. Admittedly, it might have been too cumbersome to bring a wide array of lay voices into the actual sessions at Dallas, but the bishops were not totally bereft of logistically manageable options for lay input. The whole experience might illustrate for the bishops the mistake made when the National Pastoral Council was allowed to disappear. That body, which had significant lay membership, might have been of great assistance. Its commission had been precisely to offer wise counsel to the body of bishops on important issues of church life.

The second way in which the Dallas meeting reinforced the clericalism of the system is that it situated the issues and their responses to them in the realm of legal, and even penal, policy. In that way Dallas fell in line with the displacement which had occurred when the legal clergy had been first brought onto the stage and a new barrier against the possibility of priestly reconciliation among the parties had been put in place. It was probably too much to hope, due to the urgency of the crisis, that the Dallas gathering could have been conducted in the form of a religious, priestly retreat for the pastoral leaders of the country. Immediate, practical, and collective responses were needed in order to stem even further erosion of trust. That being said, to judge from the output of the meeting, one might reasonably conclude that among themselves the bishops acted more like a collection of division directors of a large corporation than a group of baptized brothers. One wonders if any of the non-offending bishops could have undertaken the Gospel burden of fraternal correction of those who had transgressed.

What are we to make of the outcome of the Dallas meeting? To attempt an assessment of the wisdom (much less the justice) of the measures the bishops adopted there would take us far beyond the focus and thesis of this work. Is "one strike and you're out" justice? To answer that question (assuming that the choice of a legal framing of the question is itself accepted) would require legal competence beyond this writer's ken. Besides, it is quite possible that no one is in a position yet to judge whether or not the policies adopted in the charter approximate the ideals of justice—for the victims, for the alleged perpetrators, or for the body of ordained ministers as a whole. Much will depend on the ways the norms are applied in practice.

And perhaps much more will depend on the unintended consequences that follow upon that implementation phase. Humans being fallible, even with the wisest discernment our actions always create consequences we neither anticipate nor want. Given the haste with which the bishops felt they had to act in order to address the scandal, the probabilities of such surprises are all the higher. As just one example, we might focus only on one of the relationships in the system: the relationship between bishop and priests. Have the policies in the charter erected a barrier of mistrust between the ordained and the bishop they had previously been taught to see as a caring spiritual father? One hears rumblings to that effect when priests gather. Or was that traditional view itself a piece of sentimentality supporting a less-than-adult relationship? Only experience will prove whether the concerns are founded or not. It will depend on whether the individual ordinary is able to demonstrate his commitment to two responsibilities simultaneously. One is the oversight responsibility imposed on him by the specific demands of the charter. The other is the mandate to relate to the individual priest sitting in front of him—accused but appropriately presumed innocent—with the solidarity and compassion demanded by the Gospel. Will he take up the cross of priestly (not merely clerical) solidarity or simply wash his hands and dry them on the towel of the rules? Will priests be too quick to interpret the actions of their bishop as those of an impersonal bureaucrat when he believes he is only trying to protect the innocent? Perhaps we need to simply let go of the concept of the bishop as the *father* of the body of priests altogether, and replace it with the biblical image Cardinal Bernardin used in his initial meeting with the priests of Chicago: "I am Joseph, your brother." Jesus did, after all, tell us to call no man "Father" (Matt 23:9). Such a change would not eliminate the notion of accountability; it would transform it to the *mutual* accountability implied in hallowed Christian (and priestly) tradition of fraternal correction. The restoration of trust will exact a heavy cost on all of the ordained.

The same question needs to be addressed in the area of bishop-to-bishop relationships. A quite traditional notion in church history speaks of reform and renewal *in capite et membris*. It is closely related to the repeated insistence in this work on collective responsibility for cultural transformation: to be effective, cultural transformation must involve equally both "head and members." In historical usage the "head" referred ordinarily to the pope and/or the Roman curia. In the present setting it would seem reasonable to apply the language at the parish level to pastoral leaders, and at the national level to the corps of bishops responsible for guiding the local churches in the U.S. Since Vatican II much has been made on the *conceptual* level about the collegial character of the episcopacy. As far as I know, that powerful concept has never been translated into the behavioral expectation of an individual bishop to a brother who shares the same burden of spiritual responsibility for a gathered body of the faithful. In practice, bishops remain totally independent agents, each one serene in his own fiefdom. How differently might the story of abuse have turned out if individual bishops had related as priest-to-baptized-priest and called one another to account when the first hint of inappropriate responses to instances of abuse surfaced? Is it unthinkable that bishops be challenged to that level of (non-legally-mandated) faith-sharing with a small body of their peers? I am reminded that in the '70s Bishop Topel of Spokane challenged the bishops of the Northwest to make the full thirty-day directed Ignatian Spiritual Exercises together. The result was an era of bishop-to-bishop relationship that transcended the corporate model prevalent in other areas of the country. It did not by itself prevent the occurrence of poor leadership, but surely it more closely approximated the Gospel foundation on which further collective commitments could be built.

With respect to the laity, the response of Dallas focuses totally on measures for preventing future abuse. As we will see, it provides no deeper analysis of the cultural patterns that enabled the abuse in the first place.

Whatever the eventual impact of the charter, a Rubicon of sorts was crossed. Markers were laid down. If the charter was at one level an ending, in another sense it was only a beginning. The end of Act Four left the audience and indeed the players wondering: How will it play out? It is the question at the heart of the act in which we are still participating: Act Five.

Act Five: Implementation

After the curtain goes down in Dallas, it rises on a split-level stage. On one level, the national stage, are those organizational bodies playing the roles delegated to them by the charter. They are the oversight and auditing structures charged with gathering data that might establish whether individual dioceses and bishops are honoring the commitments made by the episcopate as a whole. It's worth repeating that, even at the level of external controls, like any other policy statement the charter by itself changes nothing. Everything depends on those charged with implementation. Because there is in practice a spectrum of views held by individual bishops regarding the binding force of decisions of the corporate body, the record has apparently been spotty. At one extreme, we see Bishop Bruskewitz of Lincoln, Nebraska, simply contesting the power of the episcopal conference to mandate any form of compliance with the charter. (It raises a fascinating question: How will he deal with the fact that ratification by the Vatican has now given the charter the weight of particular church law?)

The other platforms are local in nature. The audience witnesses the drama of particular dioceses in tense struggles with their local law enforcement agencies. The actual narrative varies with the different statutory norms of each civil jurisdiction.

Two nodes of contention are most in evidence. One concerns the government's access to church personnel records: Who has the right to delve into personnel files otherwise presumed to have been private? The other concerns the varying statutes of limitations: How many years must pass before a person alleging the commission of a crime has lost the right to file a claim because the trail of evidence is presumed too weak?

This act is still unfolding, with varying degrees of speed and intensity. Preliminary judgments on the substance of the questions are being reported almost daily. But more importantly, a clear pattern is emerging as to the way the issues are *portrayed* for the viewing public. As the media clergy present the picture, one easily gets the impression that the position of the diocese is automatically wrong. What is more troubling is the portrayal which suggests that the very presentation of an opposing position is itself evidence of bad faith. The dioceses are depicted as not merely disputing a legal question of statutory interpretation. That is common practice in all sorts of matters pertaining neither to sex nor to religion. With regard to access to files we read that the diocese or religious congregation is (obviously) "hiding," and what it is hiding is (unquestionably) "evidence." The possibility that the state's attorney might be "intruding illegally"—or even, to use a parallel image, "snooping" or "engaged in a witch hunt"—is apparently not worth mentioning. Similarly with the issue of any statute of limitations. Society continuously struggles to find a just balance between the rights of alleged victims and those of alleged perpetrators. It is the stuff of reasoned debate, not only in the case of sexual abuse, but in all sorts of matters. The language of the media, instead, invariably paints the diocese as using the statute of limitations to "cover up" for men who must, of course, be guilty. The possibility that it might actually be protecting an innocent individual from a life-destroying charge is usually not mentioned.

Under any other scenario, the actions of individual bishops in the conflicts in Act Five might have been seen as reasonable behavior. Conflicting interpretations and debate about competing rights are the bread and butter of life in a free society. Sadly, because of the behavior of some of their brothers in Act Two, when quite different choices were being made offstage, the field of debate is tilted now that conflicting positions are being argued on the public stage of litigation. In the eyes of a public shaped by the word of the media clergy, white miters have been exchanged for black hats. Every individual bishop who disputes a district attorney's right to files or resists changing a statute of limitations that was enacted long ago after legislative debate, is presumed guilty. This happens before the state's attorney even begins to lay out the case, and regardless of the bishop's prior performance in dealing with victims.

Reflections in the Aftermath

What are we to take away with us from the theater, we who are both audience and players in the sad drama of these recent years? As we noted at the beginning of this chapter, its full meaning will only come with discernment over a long period. But even in this early phase it is possible to name two disturbing second-level effects. Both are serious. One is internal to the church and its mission, the other pertains to secular society.

The immediate effects in the lives of individuals—of the victims, the charged priests, the perpetrators, the innocent and culpable bishops, the broader body of ordained priests, the laity at large—are tangible enough. But, beyond those, we need to ask: what has the tragedy done to the church's very proclamation to the world?

My own concern is that it will only serve to cement in the minds of both the faithful and the onlooking public a terrible but prevailing distortion of the Gospel: that the only *real* sins are those in the sexual arena. A hallowed tradition of the saints and great pastoral figures in the church's history always maintained that what they called "the sins of the flesh" were sins of human weakness, judged with greater compassion by a merciful God. It was the sins of the spirit that drew down the harsher condemnation, from the lips of the prophets through the teaching of Jesus himself. Sins of the spirit are greed, deceit, abuse of power and authority, hypocrisy, oppression of the weak. To be sure, those failings showed up in the sexual misconduct narrative. But even as a general consensus lays the graver responsibility at the feet of the bishops, it is doubtful that the story will be remembered that way. It will be referred to as "the *sex abuse* story." And it will be tied unfairly, by church people as well as outsiders, to homosexuality, adultery, and masturbation. To that whole stew of genital stuff people really mean when they talk of—shudder!—"sin and immorality." The white-collar stuff, the sins of class and social policy and structure that impoverish and exclude those who aren't insiders, will continue to be dismissed as just "the way things are." It's always been tough to get the Gospel right. The sad thing is that it's just become tougher. "That Catholic Church—all they care about is sex!" We need a serious examination of the ways in which our catechesis and preaching covertly, if not overtly, sustain this distortion of the Christian message.

As for civil society, the focus on the transgressions of the clergy will have a different but no less destructive effect. Keep the spotlight on the religious imposters and we won't have to attend to the pandemic of sexual abuse that is occurring in the homes of the rich and the poor, and in the schools and scout troops, in every city in our country. The ordained, as guilty as they are, can serve as a perfect distraction from the far more pervasive evil of family violence. It reminds me of the line of the anonymous theological wag who said that original sin is the one doctrine of the Catholic Church that doesn't need to be proven, because it's all around us. Sadly, any influence church leaders might have exerted to help society to address this pandemic has been largely squandered; in the present context pronouncements on the societal issue of childhood sexual abuse would be seen as a self-serving attempt to divert attention from our internal disarray. More healthy potential lost through prior misuse of power.

Where to Go from Here?

But enough of sin. We Christians believe in redemption and resurrection, in a creator God who continues to labor over creation. We place our trust in a word that comes down from heaven like rain to water the earth and does not return until it has accomplished that for which it was sent. A word that produces transformation of the human spirit.

We turn our attention to what that might demand of us. For unless we work to change the prevailing culture, we will fail the moment of grace which is being offered to us even in the midst of the tragedy. As with every great historical event, the full meaning of the abuse story will be disclosed only in the response we choose to make to it. We are still in Act Five, and we, the community of the faithful, are on stage before the footlights. The script assigns us a responsibility, but we will have to compose the ending.

Chapter Five

Transformation:
Re-priesting a Clericalized Church

We began our study from the mantra commonly used to account for the clergy sex-abuse tragedy. As a way of unpacking that slogan we first studied the characteristics of cultures in general and then of clerical cultures in particular (chapter 1). Then in chapter 2 we considered the challenge implied in the call for priesting on the part of everyone who is joined through baptism to the ongoing life of Jesus. In chapter 3 we saw what harm is created when clericalization is allowed to dominate the call to ordained ministry. Then in chapter 4 we returned to the original narrative and explored the way the different clerical cultures interacted and enacted the tragic drama of sexual misconduct. Now it is time to look to the future. We need to weigh some alternatives for addressing the patterns of church life which occasioned the crisis. If we are to have hope that the story will not be repeated, we need new approaches to keep children and adolescents safe from harm at the hands of the clergy.

Levels of Possible Response

In conversations with church members around our country, two distinct strategies for dealing with the sex abuse situation generally surface. One focuses on very concrete steps being taken to prevent the recurrence of acts of abuse by the ordained and other church workers, such as teachers, coaches, and the like. I would characterize this as a strategy of *preventive measures.* Boundaries are set in place and enforced to keep specific acts from happening.

A second approach takes a broader perspective and focuses on overcoming the wide communications gap between bishops and their people that was uncovered by the abuse situation. This strategy centers on models for achieving more effective dialogue between bishops, priests, and laity so that breakdowns like system-wide sex abuse might be forestalled in the future. I would call this an *organizational structures* strategy. It aims to create a culture of dialogue, moving beyond mere deterrence of particular behaviors to the fostering of shared responsibility for the whole mission of the church. Both of these strategies have legitimate objectives and should be applauded by everyone who cares for the future of our church.

The ideas we have explored in the preceding chapters move beyond these widely discussed strategies. They suggest a third set of strategies that have not yet become part of our church dialogue. I would call them a *cultural transformation approach.* But before we lay out what that might entail, we need to consider the pluses and minuses of the first two approaches.

Preventive Measures

Within the rubric of preventive measures fall all those policies and implementation steps outlined in the famous charter enacted by the United States bishops in Dallas.[1] They include such elements as enacting serious new consequences for future transgressions in this area, summed up in the phrase "zero tolerance." Then there are the other provisions of the charter: establishment of review boards; requirements for reporting instances of improper behavior; the need for training of all church workers in measures

1. An online copy of the "Charter for the Protection of Children and Young People" can be found at the United States Conference of Catholic Bishops website: [http://www.usccb.org/ocyp/charter.shtml]. Available April 18, 2007.

for the protection of children; provisions for certification that individual bishops and their dioceses are in compliance with the requirements of the charter; etc. The steps undertaken to implement these commitments have been impressive in their scope. Quite apart from the costs in compensation to victims, the monetary outlay for training of all church workers as well as teaching children how to be vigilant and recognize inappropriate behavior has been substantial. Some outside observers have even given the church high praise for taking the lead in showing other institutions in society what they need to be doing to clean their own houses. Evidently it's possible to blaze a trail simply by dragging your heels as you are pulled where you don't want to go.

Following the charter there have been further steps taken in the area of vocational screening of potential candidates for ordination, with special focus on issues of sexual maturity. The admissions procedures of seminaries have received heightened attention. (It is tempting to delve into the issue of alleged links between the sexual misconduct and homosexuality in the ordained, but that would blur the focus of our present inquiry. Clearing up the misunderstandings surrounding this issue remains a laudable goal, however. The allegations are causing deep pain in many good ministers.)

There can be no doubt that these protective measures are all to the good. What can we hope for from them? At the very least they should surely reduce the odds of future lapses in the area of sexual misconduct. With these protections in place it is far less likely (though of course not certain) that a priest or other minister in the community will transgress. And that is a significant benefit and accomplishment. In that sense such measures are analogous to those that society generally takes to protect the innocent: the whole criminal justice apparatus of officers, jails, fines, and other constraints on criminal behavior. In effect, the church is cordoning off those people in the church community who have pathological fixations on children, keeping them from contact with our young people.

As good as such a result is, however, the preventive approach does not deal with the deeper patterns that made it possible for these crimes to occur or, especially, to be dealt with so poorly. If those deeper patterns are left untouched, they will continue to engender other less-than-salutary consequences in the church. Those manifestations may not come in the form of sexual misconduct, but they will still result in abuses of power. And that is what professionals in the field have told us the abuse was all about in the first place.

Reform of Organizational Structures

The strategies aimed at producing greater dialogue between the laity and their ordained brothers, especially the bishops, attempt a deeper cut into the traditional ways by which the church seeks to ascertain the will of the Holy Spirit. They challenge assumptions, not only about sexual deviance and the behaviors it gives rise to, but also about the whole wisdom-seeking apparatus of the church, if you will.

These take the form of calls for greater dialogue and consultation of church members on all levels: parish, diocese, regional, national, and international. They challenge the prevailing assumption that ordination, whether to the presbyterate or the episcopacy, confers the gift of unerring wisdom on questions at least of pastoral care, and even of doctrinal development.

Once again, any gains in this area will be all to the good. It is a truism in modern secular life that a community increases the possibility of greater wisdom in its decision making when it broadens inclusion in the process. Relying on the isolated and inevitably biased questioning of even the smartest leader is not a healthy formula for any organization. There is no reason to doubt that the same principle holds good for the body of Christ as well. The trust involved in developing more inclusive listening and discerning structures—all that is encapsulated in the phrase "shared responsibility"—can only enhance the adult commitment and solidarity of the church.

However, a strategy which relies only on reform of organizational structures depends on the attitudes that participants bring to the dialogue. Gandhi was surely one of the wisest students of effective collective action, and he was known to say that structure can never create character. Where bishops or pastors with a collegial orientation have entrusted significant discerning power to pastoral councils, experience has shown that much good can be achieved. But it all depends on the priestly—not clergified—orientation of the participants, whether lay or ordained.

Once more, a concrete experience helps to make the point:

> A diocese had a diocesan pastoral council composed of one-third ordained clergy and two-thirds laymen and laywomen. It had functioned very effectively in giving counsel to the bishop on significant questions of church life, counsel which informed his decision making in a substantive fashion. The time had come for replacement of some members, and I was involved in leading a process which would bring the new members into full inclusion and empowerment with the continuing members. All the members were asked to tell the collective body their sense of the immediate priorities that should be addressed by the local church. Individuals offered stimulating and sometimes conflicting ideas, the raw material for good communal reflection. Then one of the newer members, an elderly gentleman, said, "I'm here just to find out what the bishop wants." It proved to be impossible to move him away from the clericalized mind-set, with the result that his three-year term on the body was a total waste, besides being a drag on the rest of the members who took seriously their responsibility to provide independent thinking for the bishop.

A Third Approach: Cultural Transformation

A third approach aims at transforming precisely those deeper orientations of the clerical culture itself. That task is admittedly a large one, not to be achieved overnight. We have noted that once they are imprinted, cultures are hard to unlearn. The scripts for a changed culture, one that will not be clericalized, will be difficult to write, and harder to learn. Enacting them will take the concerted action of many players in a variety of roles. People—everyone—will have to stop playing old roles, and that can prove to be far more difficult than learning new ones. The inertia to maintain long-established roles and scripts packs great power. Each attempt at a new gesture or line—much less a whole new script—will cause awkwardness for the individual trying it on, as well as uneasiness in those who occupy the same stage but are still reading from the former script. It may even turn out that the presently privileged leaders, the ordained clergy, are the least consequential players of all, for they will soon exit stage right. More significant will be the youth, who in subtle ways are breathing in from all of us adults right now the previously established story line. If they are to participate in creating a new one, they will need adults to model a new script with new roles and new lines. Hence we must ask ourselves a painful question: as we ask the next generation to play new roles, are we prepared to acknowledge the ways each of us, whether ordained or not, has been complicit in the destructive old ones?

HEALING THROUGH CONFESSION

What are the essential ingredients of a cultural transformation strategy that might ground our hope for a better future? We look for an approach that substitutes a healthier model of church life for the pathological clerical culture that gave rise to the tragedy in the first place. But first we need to take a prior step. We can derive some insight from the role of liturgy in the conversion process.

Liturgy that is life-giving always begins with the act of confession. We are not transformed unless we first acknowledge our share of responsibility for the situation we hope to transcend. Confession does not complete the process of conversion, but it is the first step.

Throughout these pages I have repeatedly stressed that the clerical culture, like any culture, is generated and maintained by all those who are imprinted with the complex of attitudes, beliefs, and behaviors that characterize it. The common illusion is that "they" are responsible for the development and continuation of the harmful potential in a culture (whether that "they" is doctors or lawyers, scholars or the police—or the ordained). "We" (the respective laity) are its innocent victims. If we persist in that fantasy, we will continue in our long-conditioned behavior. We will recite our lines from the same old script. The personal question for each one of us is then: Am I ready to enter into the painful self-examination required to unearth and come to terms with my own complicity in the destructive patterns of the existing clerical culture? Am I, whether as one of the ordained or as a member of the laity, open to admitting my share of responsibility for clericalism? For it is only through the acceptance of my complicity that I can experience the power to enter into the process of creating a new set of mutual relations. I will not experience myself as a full agent in the creation of the new until I am able to give up my illusion of being a victim of the old.

Since the change required is a matter of personal commitment to new concrete attitudes and behaviors, no book can claim to do the job for each of us. But it is my hope that together we may be able to develop specific suggestions for the conversion process once that necessary predisposition has been accepted.

Principles for the Renewal Process

Before we review the specific programmatic steps that might be proposed for addressing the situation and building a healthier model, there are more fundamental principles to be considered and adopted. They emerge out of our reflections on the nature of cultures in general and the characteristics of a clerical culture in particular, as treated in chapter 1.

Transformation Is a Shared Responsibility

Cultures, as we have said, are the product of the story line, the roles, and the scripts accepted by the entire collection of players in the story. The first principle for change, then, is that effectiveness will require concerted effort by all the players to generate and become acclimated to a new story line, new roles, and new scripts. It will not help for the laity to say "priests and bishops need to . . ." unless that is accompanied by "we as laity will begin to . . ." and vice versa. What needs to change is *the relationships between* clergy and laity, and that is a systemic reality shaped by the interaction of both partners in the relationship.

Transformation Will Take Time

An obvious corollary of this basic premise is that the change required, since it is at the deep level of an ingrained culture, will take a long time. That should not surprise or depress us. We did not learn our lines yesterday. The culture itself was a long time forming. According to some anthropologists, it takes ten years to change laws, two generations to change behaviors, and two more generations to change attitudes and beliefs. Those who desire something different need to be ready for the long haul. Individual baby steps toward behaving differently will help, but the culture itself will shift significantly only when a large enough catalytic mass has been created to tip the balance.

Behavior Is More Important Than Concepts

A famous dictum in the field of systems theory has it that "the map is not the territory." Learning about something is not the same thing as experiencing it. To apply the axiom to our context: a culture is not a collection of our ideas or observations *about* the life patterns of a group of people; it is the reality itself revealed within those patterns. In a word, it is embodied, not merely conceptual in nature.

That means that, like the original culture itself, the changes involved in cultural transformation must be embodied, behavioral. We will not transform the clerical culture by thinking about it or even discussing it in groups (much less by reading a book). It will take place only as participants risk *acting* out of a new model.

Transformation Will Involve Conflict

It follows that the process of transformation, because it is embodied, will involve conflict. It requires individuals to risk throwing away old scripts and behaving within a new story line, actually "writing" the script as each new situation between a cleric and a layperson presents itself. That requires priesting: full presence and responsiveness to the person in front of us. Conflict is inevitable, because at the same time the stage will be populated with other people who still need the support that comes from the traditional scripts. This will be an upsetting experience for them because it disrupts the patterns that made them comfortable.

Once again, a concept from organizational theory can help us to understand what is at stake. The communications theorist Everett Rogers analyzed the process by which people adopt new ideas and the new practices required if they are to improve an existing system. He shows how new practices are gradually adopted by more and more members and eventually permeate and become new norms for the group.[2] As a result of his work the term "early adopters" is heard more frequently in our public conversation. People with different orientations to tradition and innovation respond at different speeds to new models when others begin to behave in ways that differ from the normal expectations of a given culture. One result is the increase of tension or even open conflict. As the early adopters (whether clerics or laypeople) begin to shed their accustomed attitudes and behave toward one another in new ways, the late adopters who are more wedded to the traditional can be expected to react negatively.

We saw this happen with the changes introduced by Vatican II, whether they involved changes in the choreography of the Mass or religious women handing over the management of schools and hospitals to laity. The response of those slower to adapt to change has frequently been to push back. Besides slowing the process of adoption by the church as a whole, the tension has led in some instances to acrimonious charges and countercharges.

We can anticipate that the effort at removing the disfiguring elements of the traditional ordained-lay relationship will be equally stressful and even contentious. Conversion at any level is costly. It will be more so when the patterns to be changed have been

2. See *The Diffusion of Innovations*, 3rd edition (New York: Free Press, 1983).

ideologically identified as God's will. The ordained will resist giving up the benefits they have derived from the accustomed expectations, and laity will resist the call to assume responsibilities they did not have to bear under the prior arrangement of roles.

To be very direct and personal: *we* have *all* created and maintained the clerical culture which clouds our church's proclamation of the Gospel. We have all played superior-inferior. And we will each have to work hard to unearth in ourselves the sinful dynamics at work in its continuance.

The Principle of "Best Practices"

If the strategy of cultural transformation is to succeed, it will require not only a new set of attitudes, but also the modeling of those attitudes in constructive relational behaviors. The ordained will be challenged to relate to laity differently, and vice versa. And within the body of the clergy itself, ordained priests will have to break out of their comfort zone and perhaps challenge other priests; they will have to relate differently to their bishops; and individual bishops will have to relate differently to their fellow bishops. Where will we find the models for such behaviors?

Fortunately they are in our midst already, if we can only attend to them. A growing body of wisdom in the field of organizational development teaches us that a problem-solving approach to life is not going to create the future conditions we all hope for. Problem-solving actually only deepens the hole we have already dug for ourselves. As a replacement for that mentality, what is proposed is that we look instead at those places where examples of the desired condition already exist. The elements which make them constructive can be lifted up and imitated by people in comparable situations. We study "best practices" to ask how we can replicate them. We will see a couple of specific illustrations when we take up behavioral transformation in chapter 6. For the moment it is sufficient to put in place the principle that transformation is best achieved by building on the manifestations of good practice already present in the community.

The Foundational Requirement:
Retrieval of a Common Identity

It would be tempting at this point to jump directly to the behavioral expectations to be looked for in a transformed lay-clergy relationship. That would be a mistake, if only because it would be yielding to one of the deepest flaws in our American culture. The impatient question of our society is always: "OK, but what are you asking us to *do?*" Before we examine what laypeople and ordained ministers are being called to *do* in a transformed relationship, we must anchor those expected behavioral changes in the adoption of a common *identity*. This identity building, though it will have to happen along with behavior modification, is part of the relationship focus underlying this discussion's approach to transformation. Without it, we just have another list of prescriptive measures, much like the charter. Behavior modification that does not spring from a solid sense of identity is like the shallow growth Jesus spoke of in the parable of the sower, the flashy exuberance that springs up quickly but just as quickly withers because it has no roots—like most New Year's resolutions.

There is a second, more important reason for turning first to the issue of identity. Shared identity binds people together, while behavioral expectations that are based on differing roles in the community can keep them separated. If we begin our search for transformation by first drafting one set of behavioral expectations for the ordained and then another for the laity, we could be unconsciously contributing to the very pattern we are trying to transcend. True, we will indeed eventually have to describe different sets of changed behavior for laity and for ministers. That will bring with it the risk that each party to the relationship might fall back into a pattern of focusing only on what the other guy should be doing. Every last one of us has personal work ahead of us. Only the development of a unifying identity and mission can sustain us when the going gets rough and we might be inclined to put all the responsibility on the other party in the relationship.

At issue, then, is: What is the nature of that most profound identity we are called to embrace? From what was said in chapter

3, we know it centers on our baptism and our sharing in a common priesthood. Those concepts will remain attractive but empty words, however, unless we work at the difficult personal discipline involved in changing deep-seated images and attitudes that perpetuate first- and second-class citizenship in the church.

Elements In the Transformative Process

Prayer. That discipline must begin in prayer—for the *desire* to be transformed by the Lord. If transformation is to happen, it will be the gift of the Lord. We need to pray for ourselves but also for the body as a whole. We must ask to have our attitudes converted, even though we cannot know in advance all the discomfort that such a conversion may cost.

Attentiveness to experience. Our prayer will need to be accompanied by personal work. It takes the form of conscious attention to each of our actual interactions with those in a different state within the church. We will need to reflect with questions like these: What just happened? How did I present myself? What self was I acting out of? Did I take the easy route of accepting the customary minister-layperson relationship? Or did I take the risk of letting go of that old persona and perhaps making both of us feel awkward because we didn't have the old scripts to fall back on? If I did try a new form of personal, priesting presence, what did I learn? And if I fell back into the old script, how can I catch myself better the next time?

Learning from the example of Jesus. Ultimately the transformation (like any effort at spiritual growth) will require the search to live with the mind and heart of Jesus, which is the most profound challenge of our baptism. The Jesus of the gospels resisted every form of clericalizing expectation that others operating out of the unredeemed traditions of his day tried to place on him. He refused to let people call him "master" or "teacher." He broke through gender expectations and the purity code that made individuals into social pariahs on the basis of physical infirmities. He vehemently attacked role-based hypocrisy on the part of the lawyers and guardians of oppressive human customs cloaked in pious religiosity. He refused to play the game of "gotcha," turning the tables on scribes and Pharisees whenever they tried to compel him to give answers to questions they themselves would not risk addressing. In his hour of greatest crisis, he was his own person as he stood before the high priest, choosing when to speak and when to be silent and deciding what respect for the office of high priest demanded and what it did not.

Choice of our most important identity. Whether we are pastor or layperson, we will all need to dig down inside ourselves to find where we are going to choose to identify. Identity is not a single, stable reality we possess and control. All of us actually have multiple layers of identity: think of a husband or wife who is simultaneously a parent, a member of a faith community, participant in a bowling league, and a card-carrying alum of dear old alma mater. What is at stake is a process we must constantly be engaged in, a process of *actively identifying*, of situating ourselves with a person or group of people. Depending on the level at which we identify, we relate to reality in very different ways. An example makes the point:

> A major superior of a large congregation of women religious once told me that they had just experienced a totally unexpected reversal of their situation. The state legislature had suddenly outlawed all funding for religious schools, with the result that the sisters would have to withdraw from many of them. She said, "I believe we are faced with a golden opportunity: we have seven hundred highly trained educators who are now free to teach in all sorts of nontraditional and even noninstitutional ways. The question is: will they be free to move out and try new ways? Where do they find their identity?"
>
> I once told this story to a group of educational administrators. I said that any of those sisters might find her identity as a Catholic-school teacher and be incapable of functioning except in that setting. Or she might identify as a classroom teacher and be comfortable wherever she might find a classroom. If she identified at a still deeper level she might identify herself simply as an educator and be able to find any number of nonschool settings where

she would continue the educational process with whoever sat on a log with her. When I finished the brief input one of the participants, a college dean, said, "You have just named my problem! What do I do with the guy who has apoplexy if I move him from Room 101 to Room 102?"

We will have to ask ourselves: Where do I find my Christian identity? Do I find my primary meaning as a Christian in my canonical status: as a layperson or a designated minister in the community? What is more important to me, that I share with all these people in my church community equal membership in the pilgrim body of the risen Christ—or that I dress this way rather than that, am addressed this way rather than that, hold this place rather than that in the ordering of the community's life? What level of identification is primary and makes every other distinction quite secondary?

The task of identifying above all with the priesting presence of Jesus, of relating to my neighbor as person, is incumbent on every one of us, whether ordained or lay. It names the one journey common to us all, on which we are responsible to help one another, not as keepers but as brothers and sisters. It is only to the extent that we assume that identity at the deepest level of our psyche that we will be able to respond as mature adults to the appropriate distinctions of role within the church community, neither abusing them by assuming an attitude of unwarranted superiority nor allowing them to turn us into spiritual adolescents.

With these general principles for cultural transformation in place, we can turn our attention to what will be required if the particular relationship between ordained ministers and their lay counterpart is to be transformed into the priestly reality called for by their common baptism. The principles set forth in chapter 5 ground a strategy which aims, not merely at prevention of abuse or even at the development of collaborative organizational structures, but at cultural transformation of the church community. In the next chapter, we'll see specifically what we might do to revise our Christian identity and relationships in ways that reflect priesting rather than clericalism.

Chapter Six
Expectations of the Ordained and the Laity

Having looked at the principles that will underlie true transformation of the clergy-lay relationship in the church, it is time to ask that question we love: What then should we *do*? One of the things the abuse crisis has done is awakened us to destructive and damaging patterns. Working through this current discussion gives us another way to approach our role in both the culture that gave rise to the scandal and some ways to guide the transformation. Assuming that everyone in the Christian community is called to work at putting on the mind and heart of Jesus, we can identify new behaviors that might be called for from each party in a transformed clergy-lay relationship.

First, do we begin with the ordained, or with the laity? Given the hope that it is to be a relationship of peers, there is no intrinsic reason why we should begin with one set rather than the other. But our conversation is by way of a book rather than face-to-face, which means that the author happens to be first to the keyboard. So I'll make the call by starting with the ordained. But if I may offer a humble suggestion to the reader, it would be that you read first the section that applies to your own status in the church. After you have listened to the suggestions there (and perhaps challenged them, or bellowed with rage at my hubris in proposing them—and perhaps even brought them to prayer?), see what might be expected of your partners in a different, but related state. (Expectations of the laity begin on page 133.)

Expectations of the Ordained[1]

We are not without ordained priests who model the kind of relationship needed for transformation of our clericalized church. Ask most laypeople and they can immediately point to particular priests who continue their life of priesting in spite of the potential for clericalization inherent in their clergified state. What we need to do is to lift up their "best practices" and figure out what makes them so effective.

The most obvious component is the evidence given by such ordained ministers that they are aware that they are on the same faith journey as those to whom they are called to minister.[2] The same beatitudes challenge them; the same weaknesses bedevil them. They do not have to pretend to some sort of achieved state of holiness conferred on them by their call to ministry. Their faith is lived in the face of question and doubt. They walk the same way, challenged by the same Jesus who called himself the Way. For them Mary the mother of Jesus is not the example of other-worldly purity, but rather the first exemplar of a life based on faith.

1. In the discussion that follows, although our main concern is the ordained clergy, it should be evident that the proposed changes apply to anyone called to the particular pastoral role in question. DREs and youth ministers can be just as afflicted with clericalism as the ordained.

2. Kenan Osborne provides good historical data on the post-Trent struggle over what was to be taught about effective priestly spirituality. The work of Jean-Jacques Olier, which became the *vade mecum* of seminarians for centuries, was revised by Olier's own Sulpician superior Tronson without Olier's permission. As Osborne notes: ". . . the image of the priest in Olier's writings was essentially pastoral, baptismal, and mystical, while that of Tronson was clerical and ascetic. Olier had emphasized the pastoral dimension; Tronson, the ascetic dimension. From 1676 to 1966, it was Tronson's view that dominated the seminary system. *The priest was a man apart and a cleric separated from the laypeople. Seminarians should be trained to keep themselves distinct from laypersons and separate from the spiritual life of ordinary Christians.*" "Priestly Formation," in Raymond F. Bulman and Frederick J. Parella, eds., *From Trent to Vatican II: Historical and Theological Investigations* (New York: Oxford University Press, 2006), 125. (Emphasis added.)

All these things they share with the rest of the baptismal priest-hood, to be sure. As we saw, ordination does not bring about changes in personal holiness. But entry into the clerical state does bring with it a new set of *expectations*. The ordained become public persons in the church. How does that fact add further specification to the general call to holiness that is incumbent on all the baptized? Perhaps we can put the question this way: In a transformed, de-clericalized culture, how do the beatitudes which challenge each of us translate into new behaviors the faithful might rightly expect of our ordained priests?

I would suggest we might profitably look at four expectations of the ordained priest: proclaiming the Word of God; presiding at the public worship of the community; providing guidance to individual Catholics in their spiritual lives; and leading a Christian community on its journey of faith.

1) Proclaiming the Word

The first thing that the community of the faithful rightly expects of its presbyters is that they engage the community with the Word of the Lord. That responsibility situates the presbyters with feet in two distinct worlds, because the Lord's Word is spoken in both the Scriptures and in the community's contemporary experience, the signs of the times.

First, the Scriptures. The priestly responsibility arising from baptism requires of every Christian that he or she personally hear and ponder the biblical call to conversion. What the community expects of its leader, and rightly so, is a reliable guide on that journey. A wonderfully evocative phrase calls preachers and teach-ers to "break open" the Word. It is as if the Scriptures were a rich loaf in their hands, ready to offer sustenance and life for a people hungering on their journey through alien territory.

But the metaphor breaks down when we realize that you can't "break" this kind of bread without having first tasted what it has to offer yourself. Much has been written about the need for solid homiletic training, and that must not be discounted. But, as we learn from all the arts, mere technical competence will never of itself beget a work of art. What counts above all is the interior, the mind and the heart, of the artist. In this case the art is to break the bread of a word that has become flesh in the preacher's own experience. It means doing it in a way that evokes in the community a hunger they may not have even been aware of, and then satisfies it. It is not ultimately a matter of rhetorical eloquence. As Paul in 1 Corinthians emphasizes, if love is missing, the eloquence even of an angel produces nothing more than the hollow sound of a gong (1 Cor 13:1-3).

That means the proclaimer must enter into the drama of God's people as they make their way across the centuries covered by the Bible. For what is going on in life *is* a single story beginning with the account of creation and continuing in the ongoing drama in which the hearers of the Word are participating right now.

The preacher is not merely telling the story, the way a parent might tell a bedtime story to a child. The servant of the Word must also be engaged as one of the participants in the story. Preachers are not there to "teach" those who are ignorant, to "tell" it or pour it into empty ears, but to *engage them in their own history* as it is being lived by the people in the Scriptures. To do that, presbyters must allow themselves to experience what that people is going through. It means entering into the consciousness of Mary as she "pondered in her heart" the painful role she was being asked to play in that amazing drama of sin and liberation. And above all it means entering into "the mind and heart" of Jesus, taking on what Jesus experiences as he enacts his own incomparable part in the story. It means crying out in real hunger; challenging a God who has a deaf ear; acknowledging our helplessness in the face of powerful enemies; and shouting in triumph at the victories of the Lord. It means that the Scriptures must be for the preacher not a book of recipes for soothing or even for moral guidance. The words must burn and sting and confound and convict as much as they inform. The psalms are not Hallmark cards to soothe the faithful.

One implication of this demanding presbyteral role is that a homily should only rarely (if ever) contain the word "you." "You" language is clerical: someone who already possesses the truth telling those who need to hear it. The preacher who is priest and not merely the conveyer of clerical-church talk must stand within the circle of those addressed. This preacher is not some oracle standing above the congregation and telling the people what "they" need to do. A homily should be a "we" experience. The word of the Lord is coming to *us*, a *people* always in need of fuller transformation, of deeper conversion. The preacher just happens to be the one standing in the middle and using the microphone. The Word is to support—and question and disturb—the presbyter as much as any other member. The preacher who stands within the story will feel in his bones the anguish of David when he hears the shattering word of Nathan: "you are the man!" (2 Samuel 12:7). He will know the pain of Peter when Jesus has to ask him for the third time, "Do you love me?" (John 21:17). And he will know the exhilaration in the voice of the beloved disciple when he realizes that it was the risen Jesus who had called to the fishermen from the shore of the lake: "It is the Lord!" (John 21:7).

The issue becomes more complex when we realize that the word of the Lord reaches us also in the daily movements of our human experience. The preacher must not only be a hearer of the word in Scripture, but must also let that word crash against the cacophony of our present human song. A homily that does not compel its hearers to wrestle with the deeper meaning of the rumblings at the core of our evolving world is a form of cotton candy. The priestly proclaimer of the Word in Scripture has to be a reader of the Word in the world as well. In Karl Barth's famous image, the preacher must preach with the Bible in one hand and the daily newspaper in the other. (That complex task becomes even more challenging when your newspaper is the Sunday *New York Times* instead of some village Blatt.) The Lord who tells the story in the Scriptures questions the story of the Lord on the street, and vice versa. The preacher who is listening to only one of them is failing the people.

Once again we come up against the risks of the clericalized cocoon. Separation from the struggles of daily living and the de-

mands of day-in-day-out loving can shrivel a human being into a
bloodless functionary. There is another irony in play here. We have
noted that one of the operative assumptions by which the clericalized minister shuts out reality is by asking dismissively, "What do
the laity know?" All too often the laity find themselves asking,
"What does this guy really know about our world?"

When one of the community's priests is called forth for ordination, that member is not being called to leave the world but to
bring an ever richer sensitivity to the ways the Lord is at work as
he or she enters more thoroughly into it. The widows and orphans
and aliens, the pharaohs and scribes and Pharisees, the tax collectors and prostitutes, the Pilates and Marys and Zacchaeuses—
these are not cardboard cutouts from a Sunday school workbook.
They walk our streets.

The minister who is not wondering publicly how power is being
used right now to oppress those on the margins in our world is offering the people half of God's word. (Actually, less than half, because even the Scriptures being used have been transformed from
bread into the cardboard of apolitical moralizing.) Unfortunately,
many of the people in the pews have imbibed a catechism of avoidance which tells them that real social issues are all "politics" and
have no place in church. Vatican II's bracing teaching in *Gaudium
et Spes* is still too threatening for some pulpits. The joys and the
hopes, the sorrows and anxieties of people around our globe are
the call of the Lord to us, challenging us just as the Lord identified
with the Christians being persecuted by Paul (Acts 9:4).

Presbyters following "best practices" invite laypeople to pray
and reflect with them as they challenge the community to see what
the Word is asking of their community during this moment of
world/nation/city/neighborhood life. And healthy laypeople will
ask to join their ministers in that task.

2) Presiding at Common Worship

The liturgy is the primary place at which the presbyter joins
the life of the faithful to the ongoing story of God's faithfulness

in the face of our infidelity. In the holy priesthood's common worship, the ordained minister is called to preside, to call forth the prayer of a single unified people.

When it comes to the ordained minister's liturgical role, the first thing to be observed is that I did not say the priest is to act as the "celebrant." It is not the ordained minister who celebrates but the gathered faith community. The community of the holy priesthood celebrates as a single body. The minister leads by evoking the Spirit of prayer from the heart of the congregation. If we do not remind ourselves to use more accurate language to describe what is actually going on, the language itself will continue to contaminate our efforts at transformation. It will require a profound conversion for some priests, and the members of their communities, to realize that the priest is presiding not *over* but *within* the collective act of the assembly. The priest is not performing a ritual that the faithful merely observe or listen to. Traditional Scholastic theology, in its effort to define what makes the ordained presbyter essentially different from the layperson participating in the same liturgy, declares that the presbyter is the only one who is able to "confect the sacrament." That is a perfectly correct answer to a question that has been framed in terms of *sacred powers*. But it does no service to our church's message about the dignity of the baptized community of priests. A priest who presides at liturgy in such a way as to communicate, in effect, that the laity are merely in attendance at his act of "making Jesus really present" is actually obscuring the profound truth of the risen Lord's presence in the lives and worshipful gathering of the priestly people.

That said, what should the community rightly expect of its liturgical leader? And, in light of the main focus of our reflection, how might the reality of clericalization affect the fulfillment of that expectation?

The simplest way to say it is that a community has a right to ask that, for its leader as for each member of the community, the liturgical experience be one of *prayer*. That does not mean saying prayers or reciting the canon, but praying. The community will be challenged to enter into an act of common prayer to the extent that the leader is actually *engaged in prayer*, that is, standing in the presence of the Lord in the present, at the moment.

Whole libraries could be filled with the volumes written about the priest's need to be a person of prayer. The pious exhortation is usually cast in terms of the struggles and difficulties, or even the temptations, to which the priest will be subject in ministry. In other words, they're about his private prayer life. Candidates for priesthood are often told: "If you aren't a person of prayer, you won't survive in the priesthood." When you think of it, the caution doesn't really add anything to what is true and expected of the baptized. If we aren't people of prayer, none of us will "survive."

Rarely, if ever, will you see any reference to what the liturgical leader is doing in the actual process of presiding. There is a connection between prayer in private and leading the community in prayer, of course. Someone who is not a person of prayer in daily life will not become one upon processing up the aisle. What calls for further reflection, however, is the behavior taking place, not in one's cell preparing for worship, but in the liturgical action itself. The issue then becomes: Does the presider give any evidence that he or she is standing naked in the presence of the All-holy One, the one whom Jesus calls "Father?" Is there any awareness that the presider is standing in the midst of the "great cloud of witnesses" of the letter to the Hebrews? Does the community experience here a person who is caught up in praise, or crying out for mercy, or chastised by the challenge of the prophets? Do they see the presider's joy at the awesome gift of liberation? Do they see someone identified with Mary, simply lost in sheer wonder at the magnanimity of our God? How?

We're back at embodiment. At physicality. At the sacrament of the body-person mediating the experience of standing in the presence of the Lord. Presiding is an embodied act of communication with and within a praying community. What does it say if the congregation never sees a smile or a tear on the presider's face; if the presider's hands never come within a country mile of clapping; if the presider's body never moves or feet never tap to the beat of a joyful song?

One of the most common complaints people in the pews make about presiders is the poor quality of homilies. And there is plenty of evidence to back it up. But I have also sat in the pews and heard the priest give a really fine homily—engaging, solidly based in Scripture, dealing with contemporary issues of great importance—only to have him end the Liturgy of the Word and continue: "TheLordbewithyou," "Liftupyourhearts," "LetusgivethankstotheLordourGod." What follows is a runaway train rattling on to the end of its run. The recitation might be in the vernacular, but it could just as easily be in Sumerian and nobody would notice the difference. Cognitive meaning, not to speak of affective engagement, have fled the building with the final word in the homily. The disconnect between the challenging homily and the mechanized aural assault on the eucharistic prayer apparently escapes the notice even of many priests who are otherwise very pastoral in their dealings with laity. The faithful in the pew are called to be a community at prayer, but the way the prayer is proclaimed is crucial for that.

The call for a presider genuinely to be praying while leading the congregation at worship runs counter to the tendency of clericalization, which promotes rote performance, statuesque impersonality, and a deadly focus on correct choreography, on prescribed rubrics. What is communicated when the primary concern of the altar servers at Mass is fear that they won't get it right, rather than joy at being at home in their Father's house and participating in an act of praise? Does the congregation ever see a presider say a quiet thank-you to the servers who wash his or her hands? Do communicants ever see the presider smile as they share in the most intimate act of joy imaginable, the handing over and receiving of the bread of life? The minister is not dealing from a deck of cards, after all. Does the experience reveal the face of the Jesus who said, "I no longer call you [servants] . . . I have called you friends" (John 15:15)? And "I have told you this so that my joy may be in you and your joy may be complete" (John 15:11)?

One of the manifestations of clergyhood is the expectation that one will adhere faithfully to a set of prescribed ways of doing things, to rubrics. What is rarely spoken of is the built-in tendency of oft-repeated rituals to become routine and, quite frankly, dead. Instead of being sacramental (read: priestly), routine liturgy becomes the counter-sign, the anti-sacrament if you will, of what the ritual is attempting to express. The rubrics are followed exactly as prescribed in the book—while the faith of the faithful is being stretched to the breaking point by the dullness and impersonality of it all. The Catholic dioceses of our country expended significant money to hold all those workshops on the General Instruction on the Roman Missal (GIRM), focusing on ritual correctness; it might have been better expended on efforts at getting the presiders in touch with their humanity. That is the essential component of priesting.

The leadership and the primary (though not the sole) responsibility for generating the attitudes of the prevailing culture rest with the clergy. It is they who have taught the laity how to behave (a teaching the laity have been content to acquiesce to, we must remember). In the ordinary run of things it will be the clergy who will have to take the initiative in creating its replacement, though assisted, as we shall see, by the laity in shared responsibility. It is the presider's inner spiritual journey coming to expression, the presider's vulnerability, that is the key to the congregation's response. That's scary stuff because it calls into question whether the one proclaiming the exalted words really believes them. It challenges the presider to be present to what God is doing in him or her, to make that experience present to the co-worshipers by bodily expression, in order to evoke their presence to the Lord in turn. As we saw in chapter 2, it is presence to the fullness of reality that is the Gospel demand incumbent on all the baptized. For a liturgical presider, that means affective presence to the drama of the moment. When the ordained minister is preparing to process up the middle aisle at liturgy, a reminder of what he or she is being called to do is needed. The inner dialogue might run like this: "I have done my part in lining up the ministers for this procession. If they don't all bow at the same time it is of little matter. Whether the altar servers are ready with the bowl for washing my fingers, likewise. Whether the eucharistic ministers all get to their right places, likewise. I am about to lead this community into the presence of our common

Father with the offering of Jesus in our hands. Nothing else is worth my attention. Lord, send your Spirit to take hold of me and compel my attention through this Eucharist with your loving presence, so that my prayer may call forth the prayer of your people."

It's not easy, week after week, liturgy after liturgy.[3] The tendency to clericalization and routine make it a demanding challenge. But it is really only a further explication of the charge given by the ordaining bishop as he hands over the paten and bread to the candidate for presbyteral ordination: "Receive the oblation of the holy people, to be offered to God. Understand what you do, imitate what you celebrate, and conform your life to the mystery of the Lord's cross."[4]

3) Guiding in Matters of the Spirit

The third gift the community of priests seeks when it calls forth some members to minister to it is the ability to accompany individuals as they attempt to discover the workings of the Spirit in their lives. A personal story helps to create a context:

> I have been lifelong friends with a Jewish-American couple who are very active in U.S.-Israel relations and were personally close to prime minister Yitzhak Rabin. Both were outside the country on the day of his murder. Upon returning to the States, the first priority for each was to go to his or her respective rabbi. Deeply shaken, they turned to a revered religious wisdom figure to seek out where God might be found in the midst of this senseless tragedy.

I asked myself and I invite my reader to ask: how many highly educated Catholics would turn to their pastor for guidance in a similar situation?

The time when an uneducated laity needed an ordained minister to explain the bare fundamentals of the faith is long past. Laymen

---

3. For a fuller treatment of this issue, see my article "Is Creativity in Song Enough?" *National Catholic Reporter*, August 27, 2004.

4. *Rites of Ordination of a Bishop, of Priests, and of Deacons.*

and laywomen in our developed society are educated to levels their grandparents could scarcely imagine. To be trusted to provide spiritual guidance in the complex world faced by today's adults requires demonstration of a high level of sophistication. An incident that took place during Vatican II focuses the question for us:

> I was studying in Rome at the time. It was customary to invite distinguished guests participating at the council to dine with our religious community. One evening we were treated to a conversation with one of the Protestant observers, the Yale theologian George Lindbeck. The discussion turned to the kind of situation we might be facing when we returned home after the council. One of the wise futurists in the group ventured the observation that perhaps the biggest challenge we faced would be the emergence in the coming years of a well-educated laity. How would our seminary-educated clergy be able to stand as peers with such a congregation? It was indeed a disturbing prospect.
>
> Someone in the group, perhaps as a way of containing his own apprehension at the situation, ventured a suggestion which might make it less threatening. He said, "We need to remember, however, that although the laity may be becoming more educated in general, they won't be as educated in theology as the clergy are." Lindbeck listened attentively, and I have never forgotten the insight in his reply: "That may be true, but we have to remember that once a person becomes more solidly educated in any field, the person becomes more equipped to see through shoddy thinking even in a field the person knows little about."

Even the most humanities-challenged nuclear physicist will know what is going on when his pastor is spouting some theological gibberish which has passed into memory without ever brushing up against the pastor's mind. Sadly, Lindbeck's astute observation would not even be acknowledged in some of our seminaries forty years later.

Spiritual guidance requires finely honed sensitivities. It is not a question of teaching (much less of giving people the pat answer of a numbered paragraph in a universal catechism), nor is it a matter of providing nosegays. The listening skills alone that are needed require training and mentoring of a high order, not to mention the further discernment needed to interpret what one is hearing and what it means for the struggle going on between the spirits of light and darkness.

At an earlier era the priestly community of the baptized would have looked exclusively to the ordained for such gifts. One of the blessings of our day is that the Spirit has called forth laymen and laywomen who are not called to pastor congregations but who bring precisely those gifts of wise discernment to the service of the faithful. Whether they are called "spiritual directors" or "companions on the way," their gifts have been validated by the experience of thousands whom they have companioned.

This does not mean that the ordained have no role with respect to that need of the community. Although not every ordained pastor will be expected to have those gifts, they will need to appreciate their value and know how to direct the seeker to the wisdom figure who does. That responsibility presents another challenge to a clericalized mentality.

Unexamined Attitude:

Clergy: "By ordination I enjoy all the gifts the faithful need; I don't have to be dependent on the gifts of others."

In the transformed culture of a future church there will still be ordained clerics and laity. The difference will lie in the *relationship* that prevails between them. A relationship based on their common baptismal priesthood will call for an attitude not of superiority-and-dependence but of *interdependence*. Peers can recognize and respect the presence of different gifts in each other without lapsing into attitudes of superiority and inferiority. Wise clerics will recognize that some lay members have greater ability to companion others in the Spirit than they do.

And that includes the person of the pastor. Once again, if we explore already existing best practices, we will discover that a growing number of ordained ministers now entrust their growth in the Spirit to the direction of a layperson. It represents the mutuality of priesting. They need to spread that good news to others. (We may one day find our way once again to the practice of the faithful confessing their spiritual lapses and blessings to one another, without distinction between clergy and laity, and asking forgiveness, seventy times seven times.)

The priestly pastors of a transformed culture will not be threatened by the gifts of others, even in the area of spiritual guidance. They will not interpret it as a gap in their armor (an interesting image) to be called to trust the action of the Spirit in endowing lay members of the church with such gifts. The community will have taught them, through the kind of formation they receive from wise seminary formation personnel or through the proactive sharing of the priesting community, that the faithful do not expect them to be their personal spiritual guides. They look to their pastors instead to know where such gifted people are and facilitate their connection. It will take trust, but it can happen.

A competent pastor will have at his or her fingertips a list of the spiritual resources in the area: retreat centers, monasteries, and individual spiritual directors. The pastor will be listening to the experience of parishioners in dealing with different spiritual guides, and constantly alert to keep the information up to date.

4) Leading the Faith Community

The fourth gift the faith community looks for from those it ordains is leadership. To begin to understand what that implies, it can help if we first clear away some of the things the community does *not*—and should not—ask of its pastoral leader. If the laity aren't expecting every pastor to guide them with the discernment of a Teresa of Avila, they surely don't expect an Alan Greenspan either. Or a Builder Bob, for that matter.

A modern American parish is a complex human enterprise. It takes a great variety of skills to carry out its mission. The hungers of the spirit are to be satisfied with prayerful celebrations drawing on the resources of salvation history, as we have seen. But there are also classes to be taught, outreach projects to be organized, schedules to be observed, funds to be collected and managed, supplies to be bought, and facilities to be maintained. The boiler has to be watched and even trash removal takes somebody's time. Does it have to be said that those people need not be ordained? Unfortunately, from the evidence of some clericalized pastors, apparently so.

The point is, of course, that pastors who do not entrust others with these responsibilities are operating out of an exaggerated, clericalized sense of their own importance. The faith community does not call them, nor does it expect them, to do these things. And any seminary that does not disabuse its students of the self-exaltation involved in pretending to such omnicompetence is seriously failing the priestly community. Prospective pastors don't need courses in bookkeeping or facilities management, they need to learn how to elicit those gifts from the body of the faithful and then trust them when they serve the community in that way.

All of which takes us to the fourth gift the faith community rightly seeks in calling gifted members to ordination: leadership. That is, the ability to call forth and marshal the gifts of a human community moving in solidarity toward the accomplishment of a mission.

There are treatises on leadership to be found in any bookstore. Some are stirring, others banal, and others questionable as to their appreciation of what genuine human community demands (think Jack Welch). To attempt to offer one more full-blown treatise on leadership would surely take us beyond the focus of this work. Nevertheless, since the faith community does expect those it singles out for ordination to provide leadership, we need to ask what leadership in a transformed model of clergy-lay interaction might look like.

Before I describe the leadership demanded of the clergy, there is a preliminary note that I need to put in place. I had thought we in the church had moved past the need for it, but a recent conversation with a friend alerted me that there is an old bugaboo still to be cleared away. My friend was on a task force drafting a document for a committee of the bishops. In the draft of her section in the document she referred to the need for *leadership*. She was surprised to discover that her language evoked considerable resistance from the committee. Why? Because "leadership is a concept that comes from . . . *business.*"

Over my years of consulting with church organizations, I have seen displays of this schizophrenic (and unscriptural) "spirituality" that splits life into two compartments, the sacred and the secular, each existing in splendid isolation from the other. It would surface when the group was contemplating some issue in the (supposedly non-sacred) area of human resources, or marketing, or finances. It was frequently uttered with disdain: "We're a church; we're not *IBM.*" (I would have to bite my tongue to keep from responding, "No, we're certainly not. They care a lot more for their personnel than we in the church do.") So let it be said again: The church is one, holy, catholic, and apostolic—and a fully human organization. "Leadership" is not a term coming from the big, bad, secular, nasty world of *business.* It's a human issue. It is a necessary component of any human enterprise and, if it is not attended to, the energies of many good people will be wasted and the message of the kingdom distorted. It's really the point in that brief gospel parable about the owner who tried to get rid of a demon in his house. When he drove the demon out and the house was clean he discovered that he had *seven* demons, and "the last condition of that person is worse than the first" (Luke 11:24-26). Try to form a leaderless group and you will have a basket of snakes wriggling their way to domination. It's the way human beings are made, secular *and* sacred.

Mutual listening. Different theories of leadership highlight different aspects (some contradictory), but it is safe to say that, in most of them, high on the list of requirements would be the need for effective communications—on the part of the laity as well as the pastor. When that is missing you get something like the following:

> I once was asked to give a talk at a Communion breakfast for a parish women's group. I found myself seated at the head table, between the pastor and the president of the society. Since we were

the only two males there and he was the only one I had actually met before that day, the pastor and I fell into conversation while the president of the association talked with another woman seated next to her. In the course of our conversation I told the pastor of my work in organizational development. He responded, "Oh, I've read all that lofty theory. In practice it's a different story. I've asked for volunteers and tried to get these people involved, but they're not interested. They just want the church to provide sacraments for them and leave them alone."

After a bit the pastor said he had to go over to the church to distribute Communion at the next Mass, so he excused himself. The association president noticed that I was left by myself, so she turned to talk to me. She began by saying, "I couldn't help overhearing what Father was saying about us not being interested in helping. He doesn't know what we would like to do, because he doesn't listen to anybody . . ."

The two of them are accomplices in maintaining the clericalized culture. The pastor avoids having to be vulnerable by listening and potentially hearing things he'd rather not confront, while the association president settles for a state of passive resentment. Each retains the luxury of projecting all the responsibility for the situation on the other, and both dump their frustration on outside third parties instead of sharing it directly and undertaking the work of constructing something together.

A counterexample, a best practice, makes the point: A friend of mine, a laywoman, wife, and mother of a large family, was invited by the rector of a seminary to talk to the theology students on the spirituality of marriage. The students were at the internship stage, serving in parishes in their final year of preparation for ordination. They were intrigued by the kind of life experience she was sharing and the tough questions she was posing, so they asked if they could gather at her home on a regular basis for group supervision. She agreed. But she established one ground rule: "You are not allowed to bitch about your pastor." They were being called to assume personal responsibility and not go the easy route of pointing out the speck in the other guy's eye.

At the deepest level, the prime requisite of leadership is the commitment to stay at the table with the community. To stay in relationship. To confront the full reality together as peers, no matter what that reality is. As the revered apostle and pastor of the Hispanic community in the South Bronx in the '60s and '70s, Monsignor Bob Fox, used to put it, "To celebrate is to *name life.*" Reality, with its glories and its tragedies. Both the ordained leader and the members of the priestly community are called to share their experience together in honesty, whether it be the joy of the Lord's mercy and liberation or the pain of our human disappointment, breakdowns, and sin.

Attention to the health of the whole. A second foundational aspect of leadership is that leadership is always about *wholes,* not pieces. The bishop must lead the people of the diocese as a single people; the pastor must do the same for the whole parish, or for the Bible study group or the parish finance council. Individual members can care for the needs of other individual members; that is ministry. When someone is singled out from the rest of the membership and charged with leading the community, a shift in responsibility occurs. It is the leader's responsibility to attend to the human system as a whole, and that is a different kind of animal than the mere accumulation of separate individual members. A whole is not the sum of a set of parts but a reality of a different order.

> I worked once with a wonderful Hispanic bishop in the Southwest. He had been a beloved pastoral minister at the parish level. He was known for visiting parishioners in the hospital, spending time with grieving families, standing by the pregnant teenager, that sort of thing. When he became bishop he tried to replicate that model with the much larger number of people in the diocese. His staff had to teach him gradually that he could no longer function in that way. He had to become the symbolic leader of the local church as a whole. He couldn't minister to each of the hurting people in his large diocese. It was a struggle for him, because he didn't realize how much he had come to need the satisfying emotional strokes he was used to receiving from one-on-one ministry to hurting people.

If the one called to lead does not bring the energies of the community *together*, it will exist as merely a collectivity of disparate interests. Each one may perhaps be valid in itself, but without effective leadership one member will be pulling the others in ways that compete with, or even run counter to, *their* interests. In such a case, to paraphrase Yeats' wonderful words, the center will not hold. Because there *is* no center.

That means that if the leader is to bring the human energies together, he or she must be skilled at monitoring the signals the community as such is emitting: constantly listening and observing, listening and observing. Leaders must know how to interpret those signals systemically, to distinguish the ones which provide significant information about the health of the whole community from those that are only the static of idiosyncratic observations from isolated individuals. And a wise leader will not risk relying on his or her own smarts (another risk of the clericalized Olympian, as we have seen). A good leader will create forums of all sorts— whether coffee klatches or group buzz sessions or full town-halls— at which the competing sounds can be brought together. The resulting sound may be a clear and harmonious major chord, a moving minor third, or the cacophony of a catfight. In a sense the level of consonance or harmony is unimportant; the important thing is that what is really going on be genuine and named for what it is. Remember, in order to speak to the human spirit, reality need not always be the measured placidity of Pachelbel; the dissonances of Shostakovich have their own truth. To put it in more pedestrian terms, the leader (and the group) have to play the hands they have been dealt. But how it turns out is a function of the way both play them.

Admittedly, it can be risky for a leader actively to create the forum at which a complex composition might come to expression. It could be a melody that the leader might find uncomfortable to hear, perhaps even critiquing his or her own performance. It is exactly that risk that the clericalized avoid at all costs. But if the leader does not take that risk, the collectivity will never experience its full voice and become a community.

Unexamined Attitude:

Clergy: "Keep the voices isolated from one another and they'll never know their potentiality. Divide—and conquer!"

In light of the tendency in our American culture to focus on organizational structures as proposed solutions to community conflicts, it should be noted that these observations about the foundations for leadership do not imply any prescription for a single model of community decision making. When a shared experience has been acknowledged and named by the leader with the community, there still remain many ways of creating and testing options for responding to that reality. Though they differ from one another, sometimes quite radically, each holds the potential for keeping a particular community moving forward in solidarity in pursuit of its mission. One-man-one-vote decision making is not automatically the most effective. Authoritarian leadership is not always destructive; in fact, in times of crisis it may be the only genuinely caring option. And between those two extremes there are numerous varieties for consultative leadership and consensus building. The effectiveness of any model depends on the situation and need of the particular community as a whole. More profoundly, it depends on the attitudes that both the leader and the group bring to the exercise of the particular structural model being employed.

The security to trust. If it is essential for someone called to leadership to have the ability to listen and interpret the signals emanating from the community, it is another fundamental requirement of any effective leader, then, to be able to trust others. Even on the practical level, reality will quickly show the officeholder the impossibility of doing everything alone. There are just too many tasks to be accomplished.

The art and technical skills required to be an effective delegator are listed in any decent treatise on leadership, but at base the key requirement is the inner security of the delegating leader. It is the insecure officeholder who is incapable of letting go and empowering others to take responsibility for roles and tasks within the community. Note the shift in language: the term "officeholder" is quite intentional. Someone who has not received from the community the power to lead remains simply the holder of a chair: an incumbent. Leadership is not conferred automatically with the authority of office (much less with the title); it is always earned by the officeholder and freely given by a community that has experienced respect at the person's hands. Leadership is accepted on the basis of performance, not ordination or appointment to a pastorate.

Unexamined Attitude:

Clergy: "I have the title. Therefore I can expect them to follow me."

Once again we have moved into the realm of vulnerability. The clericalized pastor tries to rely on the rubber crutch of title and authority for security. An incumbent who is interiorly ruled by fear will use all his or her wits to rein in the chaos of uncertainty, and that very effort at control will only beget a defensive stance in the members. To protect themselves from a form of control that does not treat them as adults, people will tend to take one of several courses of response. Some will bury their anger at being patronized and will comply externally but with resentment. Others will act out in childish petulance, while still others will remain in the community but withdraw from any investment in the life of the group. Many simply walk away from membership in the church altogether. The point is that, whatever their response, it does not originate totally from them; it is at least in part a function of the stance adopted by the officeholder. A church community, like any other human community, is a single interlocking set of relationships, after all, and the behavior of the laity cannot help but be affected by the fear emanating from the controlling incumbent. In a succinct phrase, Edwin Friedman captures what is required of the leader: "non-anxious presence."[4] The one called to lead must, on the one hand, be *present*: engaged in the life and tensions of the community. But that presence must be exercised in a non-anxious way, emanating confidence that the people have the capacity to confront even the most complex realities constructively. Does the one called to leadership believe the Spirit *has already been poured out* or does he think he has to bestow the gift?

The Heart of the Matter is Love

We have reviewed four major hopes that the community places in those called to be its pastors. The hope that the community will be nourished at the wellspring of its own story, in the Bible and our contemporary world; the hope that its story will be joined through shared community prayer to the continuing offering of the risen Christ; the hope that its members will find in the community trustworthy companions for the discernment they need on their spiritual journeys; and the hope that the gifts of each member will be brought into solidarity with those of his or her sisters and brothers by the enlightened leadership of their pastor.

These hopes and expectations are indeed lofty. If they are to be realized it will require transformation of attitudes on the part of both the pastors and the laity. Each of the operative assumptions underlying the disease of clericalism will have to be examined and challenged. We have tried to spell out some of those changes, and the very effort of making them will doubtless reveal yet other assumptions we can't foresee now.

There is one more element on which we need to reflect. It is an element that of its nature cannot be *expected* when the church calls members to pastoral service, and yet it is the key to all the rest, the leaven which turns raw dough into the miracle of bread.

Once more, a personal experience:

---

4. Edwin Friedman, *Generation to Generation: family process in church and synagogue* (New York: Guilford Press, 1985) passim.

Some years ago the leadership at Maryknoll asked our Management Design Institute group to gather and organize data that might help them assess the effectiveness of their efforts at educating and forming their members. It involved reviewing a number of different programs carried out at sites scattered across the globe. They included initial formation, language studies, cross-cultural immersion experiences, continuing theological study, you name it.

We developed methods that gave their members the chance to articulate not only the formal benefits each program had been designed to produce but, beyond that, how it had actually affected their lives and ministry. How were they changed? What experiences stayed with them? How were they different as a result of those experiences? What were they continuing to draw upon for nourishment of their lives and ministries?

The results supplied much food for thought about the particular programs. But they brought an unanticipated surprise. They revealed something far beyond what was being looked for, something much more sacred.

To a person, the message that emerged vividly was how much they *loved the people* they served. And the love was clearly not some romanticized (and colonial) sympathy for communities on the margins of society. It was not patronizing. What was revealed was the missionaries' wonder and gratitude at the way their people had evangelized them. Several put the matter very directly: "I thought I was being sent to bring the Gospel to the people and I discovered that the Gospel already at work in them had evangelized me." Priestly people had made them priestly ministers. If their calling made them be clergy, the love between them and their people kept them priests. The mutuality of it all was palpable. And so was their joy at the privilege of serving.

Perhaps the first question in any assessment of priestly performance ought to be: Do you love your people? And for the performance of the laity: Do you love your priestly ministers?

Love is never something that can be demanded or expected, whether between a husband and wife or between a community and its leader. One day its presence is simply discovered. There.

A gift that shows up. But only after attention has been lavished and exquisitely faint whispers listened to; care poured out and self-interest transcended; and the works of mutual servanthood exchanged.

In the end we're always brought back to the challenge of the Gospel, aren't we? It is the challenge to love. A clergy that loves the people they serve, and a people who love the ministers they have called forth from their midst, will not be seduced by the poisonous fruit of clericalization. Lovers do not abuse the power entrusted to them by the beloved. This is not a pious, ethereal romance. Not pedestals and ring kissing and premature halos, but honest, shared, vulnerable presence to the raw human stuff where the creator-God labors even now. Tough love, face-to-face. The kind our vulnerable God promises.

Expectations of the Laity

In the present superior-inferior clericalization that mars the face of the priestly people, the laity are seen—and have allowed themselves to be seen—as the recipients of the good services of their pastoral ministers rather than as peer collaborators in the single mission of the Christian community. What would a transformed relationship ask of them? We will turn shortly to each of the four forms of ministry we described in the case of the ordained and ask its corresponding response from a de-clericalized laity, but first we need to examine the general effects of living for some time in a child-to-parent relation to their clergy, as second-class citizens in the kingdom, if you will.

When someone has been in such a position of lower standing and impotence and desires to move beyond it, it becomes easy to place all responsibility for changing the situation on the other party in the relationship. It can be a formula for inaction and clinging to a mantle of victimhood. The particular clergy who have taken on the role of superiors (with the tacit compliance of the laity) are seen, not as one element in a relationship, but as *the* obstacle. "*They* are keeping *us* from assuming our rightful place."

When we adopt that as the basic image we have of the other, our (unconscious) objective becomes "we have to change them." It's a misplaced and ultimately futile approach and will lead only to frustration. It maintains our sense of victimhood: we project all the responsibility on them and settle for licking our wounds instead of claiming our dignity as persons. When I was a young man my grandmother shared with me some wisdom she acquired only through bitter experience. Her husband had died of tuberculosis only ten years or so after their marriage. As she looked back she said to me, "If you ever marry, don't try to change your wife. I tried to do that with my husband and it was the worst mistake I ever made."

The reality is that the only person we can really change is ourselves. The song based on the prayer of St. Francis puts it well: "Let peace begin with me." But that painful insight of personal responsibility contains a blessed corollary: if I do really change my behavior and break an existing pattern, I inevitably change the established *relationship* (or non-relationship). My partner in the constellation is then compelled to make a decision about how to relate to the new situation I have created by my new behavior.[5]

To make the application to our present issue: laity can't change the clericalism of their pastors. They can only change the clericalism in themselves: the mindset and attitudes that they have allowed to infect and diminish the dignity of their own priesthood. It means examining the old script they have been reading from, and excising from it those components that block their growth to mature adulthood. It means developing new lines: expressions and gestures that communicate a new stance toward the person of the other.

Let's return to the notion of best practices. In the case of relationships between the ordained and the laity there exist in our midst laypersons who are already relating to their pastors on the basis of a different model, one that is energized by the baptismal priesthood to which both are called. The stories that follow illustrate individuals operating from a model of relating that is quite

5. Ibid.

different from the customary clergy-lay model. In the first we meet someone just breaking free of the earlier model and taking the risk of trying on a new one:

> The facilitating group I work with was assisting a small diocese in a pastoral planning process. We were working in a small motel that offered no space for small-group meetings outside the main assembly room. The result was that small groups were meeting in motel rooms scattered around the complex. People were sitting on the bed or on the floor around the room.
>
> One of our staff was going around and checking to see if the groups were working effectively. She came to a room where there were two priests and six laypeople. One of the priests had the floor and was pontificating grandly on some subject or other. He was droning on and on. The faces of the rest of the group indicated that they were bored and excluded and patronized—but didn't know how to change the dynamic.
>
> Just at that point the pompous cleric made a fatal mistake: he stopped for a breath. In that instant a rather large woman broke in and said in a slow drawl, "Father, let me say something. I'm just a farm woman and I don't know much about all this church stuff. But I've been sitting here thinking. And I know one thing: *I know you couldn't run a farm!* Now let me say a few things about our church. . . ." And then she let go and spit out all the things she had always wanted to say.

God bless her. She should go down in history along with the nameless woman in the gospel who broke the perfume jar over Jesus' feet (and was reviled by those who were scandalized at her indiscretion). You just know that for that farm lady the toothpaste was out of the tube and won't ever go back in. She had broken through a long-standing barrier and assumed a new form of responsibility for her life as a member of her church. It was a Neil Armstrong moment: one small step for humanity. Whether "Father" even grasped what had happened, I can't say.

It's worth noting also that she made no reference to her baptismal priesthood or any such lofty theological concept when she broke the prevailing pattern. She didn't need to. The important thing is that *she broke the pattern.* Her experience of frustration and being patronized had finally become intolerable. Her humanity required an act, a challenge that was new for her. It would not be amiss to characterize her behavior as coming from what some theologians refer to as an *instinctus fidei:* a certain pre-reflective sense of who she was and what was "right" even in the church. Without the language *about* baptism, she was acting out of the reality. She served as an early adopter. And we can guess that other laypeople in that room unconsciously filed away for future use what they had just experienced. All were changed whether they knew it or not. A new possibility had entered their church story. (And through this retelling it enters ours.)

That first tale showed us someone confronting the basic rudeness of a clericalized presbyter. He was too full of himself to see what was going on. He was "out of touch with reality" which, as we have seen, is one of the characteristics of clericalization. A second experience shows that there can be more than just rudeness at work:

John Gavigan was a committed layman who served for many years in the field of public relations for the University of Scranton. Besides his regular work at the university, he was very involved in fighting the scourge of alcoholism, long before the issue had come to the general consciousness of the country. On one occasion, after he had been reelected to the board of the local Council on Alcoholism, the new board was pictured in the city newspaper. The next day John was passing the cathedral rectory when a monsignor who was high on the ecclesiastical pecking order came out. He greeted John with a phony friendliness and then said, "Well, John, I saw your picture in the *Times* last night with your Protestant do-gooder friends." Whereupon John looked him in the eye and said, "Listen. My Protestant do-gooder friends do a hell of a lot more good than you bastards sitting on your asses in the chancery." After some huffing and shaking of the clerical wattle, the monsignor pulled himself up to his huffiest and declaimed, "No one speaks to me like that!" To which John simply said, "I'll talk like that until you begin acting like a Christian," and proceeded on his way, leaving the pompous cleric to stew in his juices. And John could do it in a way that never lessened his obvious respect for the office the monsignor held. Those he confronted usually remained friends.

Doubtless, some readers will be distressed and offended by John's "French." As noted above, new scripts will evoke conflict. This is more than the behavior of an early adopter. Some might judge it disrespectful. But was it? The monsignor was not only being uncivil, he was projecting an attitude counter to the church's message about ecumenism and was speaking disparagingly of people working for the coming of the kingdom. There is a high probability that the monsignor would exhibit those same behaviors, perhaps even more sarcastically, when in the company of his clerical circle, where no one would risk challenging him in light of his powerful position in the system. He needed to be called on his behavior. It can reasonably be asked whether a less direct exposure of the wrongness of his conduct would have had any effect upon him. And finally, the fact that he and John remained friends shows that he knew John respected his position even though John had called him on his reprehensible conduct. A different paradigm of clergy-lay relations was being embodied—fifty years ago!

And finally there is the story I once heard, of an elderly woman on her deathbed in the hospital. The young priest visiting her was doing his pastoral best. He offered her a series of pious bromides about how God would use her suffering as a way of helping others. Out of her eighty-plus years of trying to live with that God she said to the young priest, "Well, he does the best he can. . . ." How lovely: a gracious priest gently ministering to a tin-eared clergyman.

The three stories illustrate the fact that in the process of transforming a superior-inferior relationship, the one who has been in the inferior position does not have the luxury of waiting until the other party initiates the change. They also show that it is possible for the one who has been cast as an inferior to refuse that identification; to refuse to be a victim and act instead out of a deeper sense of self-worth. It requires interior work, and it might seem

futile in the short run. But the general principles of cultural transformation noted in chapter 5 remind us we're in for a long haul.
It will take one small interaction after another—both ways. In some
cases it may be a matter of the layperson simply saying, "Father
(or Reverend), I'm not here as a parishioner, I just want to talk to
you as a (sister or brother) in the Lord . . ." In other words: I'm
choosing my identity; would you like to explore yours?

Let us now turn to the four expectations identified for the ordained in the first part of this chapter. What might those areas of
ministry and the communal life of the church require for a transformed laity?

1) Commitment to Study of the Word

What is the role of the laity in the kind of transformation that
is needed if the Word is going to be seen as belonging to the entire
priesthood, not just the clergy? We noted that the Lord speaks to
us equally through the word of Scripture and the word on the
street. If the layperson in a transformed lay-clergy relationship
wants to be received as a peer in the hearing of the Word and not
merely as the one who needs to be taught, two different conversions may be called for.

The church of our time has a membership more highly educated
than any generation in its history—often more highly educated
than many clergy, as we noted above. The sad reality is that in
many instances laypeople's great advances in secular learning have
not been matched by a corresponding growth in appreciation of
the things of the Spirit. Too often we find a Ph.D. layman or laywoman with a third-grade spirituality.

It becomes reasonable to ask two questions. The first concerns
the word of the Lord who speaks to us in our everyday experience.
What will be required for our adult laywomen and laymen to undertake the serious discipline of inquiry into the spiritual meaning
of events they have come to regard as merely "secular"? And the
second deals with the Word of the Lord in the Scriptures. What
will motivate the lay members of our church to undertake the faith

journey implied in their acceptance of baptism? It will mean assuming their responsibility to deepen their knowledge and understanding of the Scriptures beyond the catechesis they received in their childhood. An approach to the Bible that reduces it to a few moral nosegays or proof-texts is unworthy of a religiously educated adult.

The layperson in a fully adult church needs to be as creative in searching ways of learning the skills of reflection on experience and growth in knowledge of the Scriptures as she or he would be in seeking out any other competence needed to function in secular society. The question for an adult layperson would be: "What steps am I taking to deepen my understanding of the Lord's message to me in the Scriptures? How can I claim to know my faith if I don't trouble myself to learn the story of my people?"

Besides exercising their priesthood by pondering God's word in their hearts as Mary the premier priest did, laymen and laywomen will have to assume the initiative by seeking out Scripture study and training in prayer forms suited to their adulthood. There are solid materials from recognized Catholic sources easily available to someone willing to take the small trouble of finding them. Laypeople who are not being helped by their pastors to a more adult appreciation of the Scriptures will need to be just as enterprising in seeking out resources as they would if it were a matter of seeking other knowledge they might need in order to function in society. Their spiritual life is surely as important as their secular competence. Although the community may rightly expect that its pastors be wise guides in helping the faithful on their journey into Scripture, it is a cop-out for the faithful to allow themselves to be held hostage to pastors who themselves have not progressed beyond some introductory courses long ago in their seminary days.

Once again we can appeal to best practices already at hand. There are groups of laywomen and laymen who have met in Bible study groups for many years on end, with their pastor participating, not as a teacher but as a fellow pilgrim. They are mature enough to see through simplistic, fundamentalist presentations of "it says so right there in the Bible" variety. They go to reputable

Catholic publishing houses knowing that they can rely on the solidity of what they have to offer. Why continue to eat spiritual cardboard when rich feasts for the human spirit are readily accessible?

And the laity of the de-clericalized church will not be afraid to ask what the Lord might be revealing through the so-called secular life of their community. They will ask themselves in every instance how the policies of their city or state or nation are affecting the "least of my sisters and brothers." They will realize that effective participation in the search for justice in social issues of the day is not something extra added on to a life of faith by religious fanatics; concern for justice, as the 1971 Synod on Justice proclaimed, is a constitutive element of faith.

2) Participation in Common Worship

If, as we saw in our treatment of what is expected of liturgical presiders, the ordained are challenged to bring their priestly, baptismal reality to worship—to stand *in* prayer as they lead the congregation—the laity are called to that same kind of personal presence in the liturgy.

This means that for their part, too, the faithful in the pew are called to be a community at prayer. Once again we meet the reality that if the liturgy is to be an experience of standing humbly before the Lord, both parties—ordained and lay—share the responsibility. There is a single human communications system in play. The whole community is the actor in dialogue and exchange of gifts with the Lord. Either the presider and congregation feed off the signals emanating from each other, or the hunger in the one is only frustrated by the arid response of the other. In his homily at the funeral of the indomitable Sister Thea Bowman, Father John Ford is reported to have made the point admirably: "There can be no spirit in the pulpit if there is no spirit in the pew."

Our stress on the mutuality of the clergy-lay relationship means that the laity, too, are called to participate with spontaneity and active presence in the liturgical action. Spontaneity does not require arm-waving exuberance or shouted Hallelujahs (at least not always), but it does require emotional presence to the words we are hearing and the gestures we are using. It calls for attention to the reality of who we are before the Lord at the present moment, as creature/sinner/betrayer/friend/beloved. It requires embodiment: upraised arms, a knotted brow, sometimes even tears. And why not clapping? Was it proscribed when we were thrown out of Eden?

Unfortunately, most of our people have been subjected to a formula-centered catechesis more suited to turn them into mummies than flesh-and-blood partners in a love affair. "Hold your hands just so." "Don't look around." Why? For fear they might see the rest of God's people with whom they are celebrating?

One of the most effective prayer experiences I ever participated in was when a presider shocked the congregation by saying, "I want you to stop on your way up to Communion and look around you at all the other sinners like you being welcomed at the table of the Lord—liars, cheats, thieves, adulterers, 'tax collectors and prostitutes.' Then let's approach the banquet table together in joy."

From personal experience I can attest to the effect it has on me, for example, when communicants make eye contact and smile as they participate in that most intimate exchange when they take the eucharistic bread or wine from my hand. Or when the community evidences some awareness of the joy or pain in the text they are singing. Or when the family of a child being baptized can let go of their church faces and engage in a relaxed, human manner in what is, after all, a singularly joyful event.

3) Growth in Spiritual Maturity

Some of what is required under this heading was treated at the beginning of this section. Claiming one's personhood by speaking up and naming one's experience, even where the effort may produce discomfort or even anger, is part of human maturity. Mature adults know how to stay at the table and show respect without backing down, as any successful marriage demonstrates. It remains for us to move beyond that foundational level to growth in the disciplines of more mature spirituality. Saint Paul, remember, speaks of putting away the things of a child (1 Cor 13:11).

Laity desirous of deepening their spiritual lives need to be proactive in seeking out resources beyond their parish community if the parish does not offer resources suited to their level of need. Most every diocese has listings of programs on things like centering prayer, guided or directed retreats, and lectures of various kinds. Admittedly, it requires effort and initiative to take advantage of such offerings. Other priorities might have to be put aside. But spiritual growth is like every other form of growth; it costs. Sitting back and expecting one's church community to assume all the initiative to care for one's spiritual growth is just another example of typical American consumerism and entitlement. We adopt it in our lives as citizens when we expect officials to take care of all our gripes but don't bother to vote or educate ourselves on matters of serious public policy; and we follow the same pattern when we go to Mass but never extend ourselves to serve the needs of the community—and then complain when the pastor doesn't do things our way.

I once observed a situation where one of the fat-cats in a parish became very incensed at an action of the pastor, even though the decision had been supported by the recommendation of the parish council. Mr. Big huffed and puffed and let it be known quite publicly around the community that he would show them by withholding his contribution to the parish building fund. A quick look by the pastor revealed that—you guessed it—his level of contributions was a pittance by comparison to his standard of living. Consumers are quite welcome at The Gap, but they won't build a church of adults.

4) Active Participation in the Faith Community

Although taking personal initiative and assuming the risk of enacting new scripts for lay-clergy relationships will be challenges for each individual layperson, the transformation of the present culture cannot be the burden of isolated individuals only. We will all be called to share a common responsibility.

Many of the faithful in our pews today were originally cate-chized into a very individualized understanding of the Christian life and responsibility. (Being church members did not free us from the downside of our American culture, after all.) Vatican II issued a profound challenge to our individualism when it pro-claimed in *Lumen Gentium*: "At all times and in every nation, anyone who fears God and does what is right has been acceptable to him (cf. Acts 10:35). He has, however, willed to make women and men holy and to save them, not as individuals without any bond between them, but rather to make them into a people who might acknowledge him and serve him in holiness" (*LG*, n. 9).

The social character of the call to holiness establishes an es-sential component for the transformation of the present clerical-ized church. We are called to participate actively in a communal journey to the Lord. We are mutually responsible to each other for the life of our faith community, both clergy and laity.

The implication of this mentality and the change of attitudes that it calls for might be best illustrated by its polar opposite:

> I recently assisted a Catholic parish in a planning project. It in-volved town-hall meetings at which individual members of the community were invited to share their hopes and dreams for the future. Every single comment was transcribed for study by the parish pastoral council. Amid many inspiring comments I noted one striking formulation: "I just want the church to provide sacra-ments for me and leave me alone!"

It would be hard to express the consumerist mentality more suc-cinctly than that. Sadly, although most would be embarrassed to put the matter so bluntly, it undoubtedly represents the mentality of many in our churches. For such people the church is *somebody else* dispensing what the parishioner wants.

It should be clear that such a "meet my needs" attitude will only serve to perpetuate the clericalization of the church. That kind of parishioner is a bundle of adolescent needs, with no sense of any responsibility to a community, treating the pastor as a depersonalized object expected merely to satisfy those needs.

If a de-clericalized church calls for ministers who have developed the skills of sensitive leadership we noted above, it correspondingly will require laymen and laywomen who are prepared to enter into the hard work of proactive collaboration in the life and growth of the faith community. Passive-dependent membership—grumbling at the nonresponsiveness of leaders while at the same time fading into the woodwork when asked to invest time and energies in the building of the faith community—won't cut it. Those who are never available for the kinds of service needed to carry out a Gospel-inspired mission—service on councils, committees, and work teams—lose their griping privileges. Responsible peer participation will require of the laity many of the same qualities demanded of community leaders, clerical or lay. It calls for the ability to listen and stay at the table when we are confronted with ideas that stretch our zone of comfort. And the responsibility not to wait for the ideas to come from the other guy, but rather to be proactive in offering constructive suggestions for the advancement of the kingdom. And the humility to put forth ideas that are not demands but gifts for the discernment and possible nonacceptance by the community. And the willingness to work at putting into effect decisions that may not correspond to one's likes but that were made in good faith. Ultimately, it will call for the readiness to put aside one's ego in pursuit of a common good.

To return to one of the foundational ideas of this whole work: the church is not a mere collection of individuals seeking their salvation through a me-and-Jesus spirituality. It is a body: a single drama involving interrelated members called to play different roles in the pursuit of a mission so vast that it calls for dying to ourselves.

Leadership and discipleship are mutual cocreating realities. A de-clericalized church will cost us all, but it promises the highest fulfillment. As Paul puts it: "[May] the God of our Lord Jesus Christ, the Father of glory, . . . give you a spirit of wisdom and revelation resulting in knowledge of him. May the eyes of [your] hearts be enlightened, that you may know what is the great hope that belongs to his call, what are the riches of glory in his inheritance among the holy ones, and what is the surpassing greatness of his power for us who believe" (Eph 1:17-19).

The Heart of the Matter is Love

When we outlined what a de-clericalized church could expect of its ordained clergy, we ended with something that can never be established as an *expectation* but is actually the *gift* which offers the only secure foundation for all the rest: the gift of love for the community the pastor serves. It is a gift to be prayed for from the Lord, with all the hunger the pastor can summon. It would be an unacceptable omission if we were not to point out the corresponding call in the case of the laity.

Beneath all the other challenges facing the laity if they are to make their distinctive contribution to the de-clericalization of the church of the future lies the call to love those who have been called to serve them as pastors. If it is ultimately only love that can enable any of us to overcome the destructive superior-inferior mindset which bedevils us in all our relationships, the principle holds true for the relationship of the laity to their pastors as well.

But what could sound like a pious ideal turns out to require a very demanding discipline. The love in question does not consist in some romanticized warm feelings. It calls above all—as all genuine love does—for honest confrontation with tough realities. The processes by which the church determines that an individual's personal sense of call warrants acceptance and ordination by the Christian community are quite fallible. The Lord's church is a community in pilgrimage, not the full realization of the kingdom. And that pilgrim character characterizes the discernment of its ministers as much as it does everything else in the church's life. Pastors, including members of the hierarchy, will be inevitably flawed. Their gifts will be diminished by human frailty and marred by personal sinfulness. If they are healers, as Henri Nouwen taught us, they will be wounded ones at best. A certain theology may

emphasize that priests act in the person of Christ, but if that notion is not balanced by the reality of their woundedness, it becomes
a dangerous ideology leading straight to the clericalism we have
been trying to understand.

It is these imperfect, sinful pilgrim leaders the faithful in the
pews are called to love. That love, because it is not sentimental,
must be tough. It is as difficult as the lifelong challenge to love is
for any married couple. It may call for moments of very uncomfortable confrontation in the face of disrespectful or even abusive
behavior; just as much as it calls for shared celebration when effective pastoring under the guidance of the Spirit brings a disparate community to deeper unity in the Lord.

It is under this rubric of love for those in pastoral positions that
we need to place the issue of *accountability*. The dominant focus of
the present work is, indeed, not on the past. We study what happened, not in an effort to redress its injustices but to discover the
patterns revealed by the past that can help us to shape a better future.
That said, it is perfectly natural for the reader to ask, "But what
about those bishops who failed the Christian community by minimiz-
ing the seriousness of the abuse and simply moving abusing priests
from one parish to another?" How might this question be related to
love for those who failed the demands of justice for the abused?

Love for our neighbor, if it is to be genuine, calls us to the difficult
practice of fraternal correction. We all bear the responsibility to help
our sisters and brothers (in this instance, our bishops) to assume
full responsibility for both the good and the destruction caused by
their actions. Simply looking away and enabling the continuation of
harmful behaviors becomes a failure of love on our part. My late
colleague and the fine spiritual theologian Thomas Clarke, S.J., offered us much wise food for thought when he pointed out that the
call for justice and the demands of love are not contradictory, they
stand together, mutually reinforcing one another.[6] We do not love if
we do not attend to justice, and we will ultimately not act justly if
our actions in the name of justice are not informed by love.

6. *Playing in the Gospel* (Kansas City: Sheed & Ward, 1986), 130–42.

To live this tension, to hold the bishops accountable but do so from the standpoint of love is a daunting challenge. It places us on a razor edge. It is just as easy to fall into a form of heartless justice that reduces our neighbor to an object as it is to practice a sentimental affection that facilitates his continued irresponsibility.

In the public, civic realm the medium for redressing wrongs is our judicial system, and it is quite appropriate for those who have been victimized to seek legal remedies for the wrongs done to them. The bishops, regardless of their holy office in the church, remain citizens subject to our law like every other citizen. Whether that approach can offer a reasonable hope of satisfaction, however, remains a prudential judgment only the victims can make. If they choose to exercise their right by pursuing that route out of love for the church they deserve the support of the faithful.

Apart from the legal order the only other available approach is for laypeople to appeal as sisters and brothers directly to the person of the bishop for admission of his responsibility. It is also the priestly step which invites him out of the clericalized realm of superior-inferior into a relationship of Christian fraternity. Experience tells us, sadly, that it offers less hope of success.

In the face of these two equally unsatisfying avenues of recourse a third option surfaces. Victims of sex abuse by the clergy, like anyone in an unjust situation, become prey to a temptation, not to seek justice but instead to call for revenge, which is quite another thing. The motives for taking action are personal to each victim or victims' advocate, but love for them requires that we speak truthfully, and the truth is that the behavior of some comes across as a call for revenge. When someone says, "No bishops have gone to jail yet" or "when are *they* going to suffer for what they did?" the shrillness of the cry comes across as more than a call for justice. Every vigilante rides under the banner of justice. When anger which was initially perfectly justified and even holy finds no suitable outlet, it can become warped into the effort to alleviate pain by striking out at those who hurt us. It is understandable but not the work of love.

This reality places on those of us who were not directly victimized (although everyone in the church is in some sense a victim) a difficult priestly responsibility toward these brothers and sisters. We must listen to our sisters and brothers; we must support them in their efforts for justice; but at a given point when their efforts prove futile we may have to help them to let go of a form of anger which is only corroding their hearts. This is not revictimizing the victims, it is helping them to use their energies on building something new. Who ever said love is easy?

The Work of Transformation Belongs to Us All

The Christian community will not be healed of the disfiguring sin of clericalism by the transformation of the clergy alone. Nor will it be made whole by the efforts of the laity to outgrow all vestiges of spiritual adolescence in them. Though we may be called to play different roles in the upbuilding of the body of Christ we are a single people, a single body, a single priesthood. Each of us, whether ordained or lay, bears responsibility for the single story of this pilgrim people. Each of us, whether we stand at the altar or in a pew, contributes by personal presence to the worship offered to the Father. Every one of us, whether ordained or lay, is called to assist our brother or sister in the journey toward holiness called for by our baptism. Each of us, whether leader or follower, is called to create the solidarity which witnesses to the unifying love of the Spirit. Each of us is called to enter into the mind and heart of Jesus, who

> though he was in the form of God, / did not regard equality with God / something to be grasped. / Rather, he emptied himself, / taking the form of a slave, / coming in human likeness; / and found human in appearance, / he humbled himself, / becoming obedient to death, / even death on a cross. (Phil 2:6-8)

Conclusion

The transformation described in the preceding chapter, as demanding as its challenge may be for each of us, is admittedly only a sketch. And one drawn on a very large canvas, at that. The empty sections within the sketch are many. To fill them in will require the collaborative effort of priests and laypeople. The best we can do about the blank spaces at this point is to point out areas and questions for further reflection.

Vocational Promotion and Recruitment

What does such a vision say, first, about the issue of vocations and recruitment? What message does the Catholic community need to be sending regarding the kind of person to be called to the transformed model of ordained ministry we have sketched? What mechanisms need to be developed in order to attract that kind of person? Where are they likely to be found, so that we might use our limited resources most effectively? Conversely, what do we need to *stop* doing? What messages do we need to eliminate and replace with others that might minimize the potentiality of clericalism in coming candidates?

What roles must parents be prepared to play, for example, as they image the ordained for their children? When I was a young priest I had a chance to visit a couple who were friends from way back in grammar-school days. The mother told me that when she was telling the children of my impending overnight visit, her young son asked, "Where is God going to sleep?" A cute story with profound implications.

A recent sad experience illustrates the power of the prevailing distorted paradigm and the work still to be done.

> As its way of promoting vocations to the ordained priesthood, a large diocese recently had a CD made to be distributed to every household. It encouraged parents to promote the idea of a priestly vocation in their sons. A friend shared it with me.
>
> A review of the CD was very telling. Nowhere in it did the words "kingdom" or "mission" appear. I believe the word "service" may have occurred once. The phrase "priesthood of Jesus Christ" recurred, but it carried a much different connotation than language about "Jesus" would have. The tone was all about privilege and status. About clericalization.

If that is what the vocational marketers are promoting in their literature, that is what our church will experience in its future presbyters.[1]

Formation of the Laity

Throughout this work we have stressed the role of the laity in collaborating to produce a dysfunctional model. Emphasis has been placed on the hard task of writing the new scripts for lay-clergy relations that will protect against the forces of clericalism. Beyond exhortations to that kind of responsibility, what kinds of formal support can the community of the church provide for those laypeople who appear ready to take up the challenge? How must the processes of adult faith formation be adapted to promote the changes of attitudes needed? Again, tough review of what we are actually communicating is in order, followed by new scripts and encouragement of those ready to risk using them.

---

1. See the earlier discussion of the image promoted in the post-Tridentine era in Osborne, page 125.

Post-acceptance Formation

It will be of no help to project a different set of images and expectations for a de-clericalized priesthood if the whole seminary process is not reassessed. To put a point on it: How have the approaches and methods of our seminaries contributed to, if not positively bred, clericalization? What would need to be changed to minimize its possibility and replace it with the ideal of mutual responsibility in and for the single priesthood of the baptized? What role should the laity be invited and challenged to play in the formation of those to be ordained in the future? Or, as one archbishop of my acquaintance was wont to muse (mainly to himself): Is a seminary the right site for the formation of our future priestly ministers? Plenty of blank space to fill in on this topic.

Other Structure and Policy Issues

Anyone who has even a glancing awareness of recent ferment in the Catholic Church will have noted by now that I have not even alluded to several hot-button issues. I have not mentioned things like married clergy, women priests, the significance of a gay orientation in priestly ministry, or the methods by which our church "discovers" (to use a neutral word) those it will call to be bishops.

Issues like these are serious and deserve the attention of wise and discerning minds. My reasons for not including them are threefold. The first was simply logistical in nature. To do justice to those valid questions would run the risk of creating a doorstop of a book. The questions noted above are evocative enough as it is. My second reason is that those questions of church policy (or even disputed church doctrine) call for expertise beyond my competence.

But on a more substantive level, I have chosen to maintain the focus on the interpersonal relations between the laity and our ordained clergy because I believe it is foundational to a healthy resolution of the policy issues themselves. If we in the church, clergy and laity alike, do not work together to uproot from our

spirits every vestige of clericalization, of parent-child ways of relating, whether at the parish or diocesan or national levels, the
benefits proposed from ordaining married men or women or persons with a homosexual orientation, or creating new methods for
selection of bishops, will profit us little. Married men, and women,
and gay people are, after all, just as subject to the allure of clericalism as our present pool of candidates. The real issue lies in the
human heart, in the call to conversion and transformation. In
putting on the heart and mind of Jesus the Christ.

A Final Word and a Dedication

For all the pain and shame the sexual abuse tragedy has inflicted
on us, we must not lose sight of the mustard sprouts of renewed
clergy-lay relations that are to be found in so many church communities across our country. The Lord has given us thousands of
ordained men and committed laywomen and laymen who work at
those best practices day after day, week after week, year after year.
Many laity have cast aside the fear that is not of the gospel in order
to minister to their ministers by naming the truth of their common
experiences. There are presbyters who are not afraid to entrust
their spirits and their very selves into the hands of their communities, with their own personal struggles, small victories—yes, and
failures—along the journey of faith. Priests all, they have evangelized me over long years and for that I am deeply grateful.

Suggestions for Group Study

Who?

Since the dominant thesis of this book has been that everyone, whether ordained or not, contributes to the continuance of clericalism in the church, the best way to engage the material would be to create a study group composed of both ordained and lay participants. At the parish level an ideal model would be for a pastor and the members of the parish pastoral council (and perhaps the finance council) to study and respond to the ideas and proposals together. If a diocese has a diocesan pastoral council, an analogous approach could provide the opportunity for significant development of a priestly relationship between a bishop and that significant wisdom body.

Those might be the ideal configurations. But that should not rule out the possibility or value of a self-selecting group of lay-people gathering on their own. Another element of the book's argument is that when laity wait for authorization from the ordained they simply reinforce the pattern that needs to be changed. Laity need no authorization to reflect and pray together in the effort to live their baptismal priesthood more fully.

Why?

It should be made clear to the participants even as they are being invited to join the effort that the primary purpose of the exchange is to assist one another in the process of personal understanding and appropriation of the material for himself or herself.

It is not to promote acceptance of the author's point of view, much less to generate a group consensus about what to do about the situation. If the participant walks away from the sessions saying, "As a result of this exchange with committed sisters and brothers in the faith I now have a richer appreciation of the complexities at stake here and have a clearer grasp of the importance I will give to possible transformation of my own attitudes and behavior," the gatherings will have achieved their purpose.

How?

Since the focus of concern is precisely that arena of personal and communal growth in holiness, it should go without saying that the whole gathering needs to be carried out in an atmosphere of prayer. That includes necessarily an attitude of extreme respect for the individual whose response differs even dramatically from that of most of the others in the group. This is a group of sisters and brothers seeking the mind and heart of Jesus, not just the town book club.

With that foundation, it's always good methodology to begin the exploration of the material by inviting each participant to begin by sharing her or his basic response to the text *without interruption by other individuals in the group*. That includes the person's emotional as well as intellectual response. Such an approach helps to create a climate in which each person feels equally included and accepted even if the person is moved in an entirely different way than others are. Focusing first on the material as a whole also helps to keep the group from being caught up and using its time on some small burr under the saddle of the first speaker. There will be time enough later to test whether the group as a whole wants to spend its time on such a point.

Once all the members have individually shared their initial responses the body as such will have a shared sense of where they converge or differ on the most significant issues, and the leader can propose that the group concentrate its efforts at uncovering the assumptions behind varying stances surfaced by the first go-round.

Questions for Reflection

How did the overall approach of the book move you? Where did you find it affirming or supporting your own prior stances or hunches? Where did you find it off-putting, unsettling, or disconcerting—or positively angering? What challenges does it raise for you personally? Or conversely, what opportunities for transformation did you find in it?

1. *The Nature of cultures*

   — What cultures have you been imprinted by that might be influencing your responses to the argument of the text? The culture of your family of origin; significant heroes or models along the way (a teacher, coach, colleague, or significant friend)?

   — How able are you to pull yourself away from the expectations of any of those cultures, to gain personal distance and form your own responses to social or (particularly) religious questions, whether your response agrees with or differs from your cultural environment?

2. *Clerical cultures*

   — What is your initial response to seeing ordained ministers placed, as "clergy," in the same category as physicians, lawyers, professors, or public safety officers?

   — How is your concept and attitude toward religious leadership and holiness affected by the ideas presented in this area?

   — How do you react to the notion that each of us contributes and shares responsibility for the continuance of the clerical culture in the church, with its positive and negative consequences?

3. *Priesting*

   — Have you ever thought of yourself and your lay sisters and brothers as priestly? What might be the impact of treating that as more than just a figure of speech?

— Do you think that treating every one of the faithful as priest would take away from the appropriate respect owed to pastoral ministers? How would you personally see those two ideas fitting together?

4. *The cultures exemplified in the sex-abuse tragedy*

— Does the story as told in the text affect the ideas and attitudes you brought to the reading of it? If so, in what ways?
— Are there elements in the way the story is told that you would agree with? Disagree with? How might you present the story differently? And why?

5. *The work of cultural transformation*

— How do the principles for the needed transformation come across to you?
— The proposal establishes a set of behaviors to be looked for from both the ordained and the laity in four interrelated areas: knowledge and investment in knowing the Word as revealed in the story of the biblical people and today's event; personal engagement in the community's liturgical life; pursuit of an ever-deeper spiritual life; and assuming responsibility for the church community. Which of those goals is more congenial to you? Which is more in danger of falling off your radar?
— In the vision presented in the section on transformation, are there challenges that cause you to plan changes in your life or thinking? Do they suggest next steps for you to take?

Acknowledgments

There is a sense in which the title page of every book, if not completely untrue, is surely at least incomplete. To say merely that this book is "By George Wilson" appropriately assigns responsibility for its message, and indeed for its final articulation, to me. But if it suggests that I am, by myself, the author, it is a poor representation of the realities of its origin and development. What follows, then, is an imperfect attempt to thank all those whose support and wisdom substantially improved both the content and the form of the work.

After reading and critiquing an early draft, my friend Jerry Pottebaum strongly encouraged me to pursue the project. And it was he who drew on his many years in the publishing business by suggesting that Liturgical Press might find that the book would fit their mission. His interest and support has continued ever since.

At various stages along the way I have been helped by colleagues and friends who read chapters and whole drafts, raising issues and questions that compelled me to take a different and more productive path. My Jesuit colleagues Brian McDermott and John Haughey, along with Jack Healey, my long-time friend and colleague at Woodstock College, brought their solid theological competence to bear. James R. Kelly looked at the book from his sociological perspective on things ecclesial and spurred me on to complete it. From a different perspective John Murray, at some personal cost to himself, was willing to retrace the personally costly experience of trying to bring a caring pastoral presence to a whole range of participants in sexual abuse situations involving our Jesuit brothers.

My friend of many years, Joe Kiernan, brought his skills as a trained sociologist and systems analyst at RCA to the table.

Other priestly friends with personal experience of the complex realities of abuse cases are Bill Donnelly, O.S.A., and from the diocesan perspective Monsignor Joe Schumacher and Father Bob Wilson, both from the Diocese of Fort Worth. I am grateful for their willingness to draw on their experience in sharing supportive reflections with me.

Gerard McCrane, M.M., is a valued friend since our collaboration on that Maryknoll planning project mentioned in chapter 6. I am grateful for his positive response to the project.

Good friend David Jamieson brought a unique ecumenical perspective from his pastoral ministry as a conference minister in the United Church of Christ, and Dennis O'Leary and Des Lamont provided insight into particular aspects of the drama.

The collective assistance of these professional and personal colleagues contributed greatly to the job of shaping the work. But even such wise and caring people could not be expected to provide the solid editorial expertise my original rough draft clearly called for.

Enter Susan Sink. I am not privy to the mysterious processes by which Liturgical Press assigns an editor to shepherd a manuscript from draft to final publication but they should bottle them. Susan was not only attuned to the nuances of the subject matter and argument of the book, she wielded her sharp editorial scalpel (ever so gently) to expose critical gaps and flaws in their presentation. A gifted teacher, she led me away from byways that held a perverse attraction for my disjointed mind but contributed nothing to the point at hand. Above all, she was able to bring me to understand the core of what I was fumbling to express. It is a feat many others in my life have been unable to accomplish.

To all, thanks, for myself as well as for you, the good readers who have doggedly traced this path and benefited from such a gifted circle of contributors.

It is customary for the writer to say at this point that any flaws in the work are of his making. In this case it is clear that even clichés can express the truth.